Vienna Travel Guide:

Discover the City of Music and Majesty on an Immersive Journey Through the Imperial Grandeur and Contemporary Culture of the Melodic Capital of Europe

Kieran Holloway

Table of Contents

Introduction

Vienna, a city that combines an energetic modern flare with its imperial past, is tucked away in the center of Europe. For our neighbors in Germany and other European travelers, Vienna is an amazing place full of architectural wonders, musical legacy, and cultural diversity that is just begging to be discovered. Vienna delivers an experience that captivates and enchants at every turn, whether you are drawn to its majestic palaces that whisper tales of bygone ages or its lively coffeehouses that ooze a homey charm.

On the other hand, one might wonder why it is necessary to have a comprehensive travel guide when going to Vienna. The answer lies in the city's multifaceted nature and the wide range of services and amenities it provides residents. Vienna is more than just a destination; it is a complex web of experiences that are just waiting to be discovered by its visitors. In order to navigate the winding streets of the Innere Stadt (Inner City) and to completely lose yourself in the sounds of Mozart and Strauss at the Vienna State Opera, careful consideration and direction are required for every encounter.

Your travel guide to Vienna serves as a compass, directing you through the city with enthusiasm and a sense of purpose, pointing out hidden treasures, providing background information, and pointing out hidden treasures. Whether you are a foodie who is eager to try authentic Viennese cuisine, a history buff who is eager to explore the Habsburg heritage, or an art enthusiast who is looking for inspiration in top-notch museums, a guide that has been carefully selected can transform your trip into a symphony of unforgettable experiences.

Additionally, due to its accessibility and close proximity, Vienna is an excellent destination for both short weekend trips and longer stays, which attracts tourists from all over Europe as well as our friends from Germany. You are urged to visit Vienna because of its numerous lodging options, well-connected public transportation system, and welcoming atmosphere. Vienna is a city that offers a unique combination of modernity and history.

Finally, Vienna serves as a reminder of the diverse range of cultures, history, and experiences that make up Europe. Vienna beckons individuals who are itching to set out on an extraordinary journey, promising an experience that speaks to the soul. So arm yourself with an extensive travel guide to Vienna, take advantage of all that the city has to offer, and let yourself be enthralled by its timeless charm.

Chapter 1:
Travel Essentials

When traveling from Germany to Vienna, Austria, or other parts of Europe, there are several essential items and considerations you should keep in mind. Here's a list of travel essentials and tips to help you prepare:

When to visit

Taking into account the weather, cost, and number of visitors, the ideal time to visit Vienna, Austria might vary depending on personal preferences and interests. To assist you in making a decision, the seasons are broken down as follows:

Spring (April to May):

- **Weather**: Spring in Vienna brings mild temperatures, blooming flowers, and longer daylight hours.
- **Cost**: Spring is considered shoulder season, so you may find more affordable accommodations and flight options compared to peak summer months.
- **Crowds**: While not as crowded as the summer months, tourist attractions can still be moderately busy, especially during Easter celebrations.

Summer (June to August):

- **Weather**: Summer in Vienna is warm. The city experiences longer daylight hours, making it ideal for outdoor activities and sightseeing.
- **Cost**: Summer is peak tourist season, so expect higher hotel rates, flight prices, and increased costs for popular attractions and restaurants.

- **Crowds**: Vienna attracts a large number of tourists during the summer months, leading to crowded tourist attractions, especially popular sites like Schönbrunn Palace and St. Stephen's Cathedral.

Autumn (September to October):

- **Weather**: Autumn in Vienna offers mild temperatures, vibrant fall foliage, and fewer rainy days. This make it a pleasant time to explore the city.
- **Cost**: Autumn is another shoulder season, offering competitive hotel rates and flight prices. You may also find discounts on tours and attractions.
- **Crowds**: Crowds begin to decrease after the summer peak, making it a more relaxed time to visit popular tourist sites.

Winter (November to February):

- **Weather**: Winter in Vienna is cold. The city transforms into a winter wonderland with festive decorations, Christmas markets, and seasonal activities like ice skating.
- **Cost**: Winter is considered off-peak season, offering lower hotel rates, flight prices, and discounts on attractions. However, prices may increase during the Christmas and New Year holidays.
- **Crowds**: While Vienna is less crowded during the winter months, popular attractions like Christmas markets and holiday events can attract visitors. It's a great time to experience the city's festive atmosphere and cultural events.

In conclusion, your choices for weather, spending limit, and crowd density will all determine the ideal time to visit Vienna. A good combination of nice weather, less people, and affordable rates can be found in the spring and fall. Summer is the busiest travel season due to its warm weather and longer daylight hours.

Travelers interested in experiencing Vienna's winter activities and cultural events may consider visiting during the winter, when the city offers a unique experience with festive celebrations, lower expenses, and fewer crowds.

Packing list

Packing for a trip to Vienna, Austria, or any European destination requires careful consideration based on the season and activities you plan to engage in. This is a general packing list to assist you in getting ready:

Clothing:

1. **Weather-appropriate Clothing**: Pack clothing suitable for the season of your visit.
   - **Spring/Autumn**: Layering is essential. Bring lightweight jackets, sweaters, long-sleeved shirts, and comfortable pants or jeans.
   - **Summer**: Lightweight and breathable clothing, such as shorts, T-shirts, sundresses, and sandals. Don't forget a hat, sunglasses, and sunscreen.
   - **Winter**: Warm winter coat, gloves, scarf, hat, thermal underwear, sweaters, and waterproof boots. Pack thermal socks and multiple layers to stay warm.
2. **Formal Attire**: If you plan to visit upscale restaurants, theaters, or attend cultural events, consider packing formal attire like a dress or suit.
3. **Comfy Shoes**: Wear dress shoes for formal occasions or nighttime excursions, and comfortable walking shoes for touring the city.

Accessories:

1. **Travel Adapter**: Pack a universal travel adapter to charge your electronic devices.

2. **Reusable Water Bottle**: Keep yourself hydrated by carrying a reusable water bottle, especially in the summer.
3. **Travel Neck Pillow**: If you have a long flight or train journey, consider bringing a travel neck pillow for comfort.

Personal Items:

1. **Toiletries**: Pack essential toiletries such as toothbrush, toothpaste, shampoo, conditioner, soap, deodorant, skincare products, and any prescription medications.
2. **First Aid Kit**: Include a small first aid kit with band-aids, pain relievers, antacids, allergy medication, and any other personal medications.
3. **Travel Documents**: Carry essential travel documents such as passport, ID, visa (if required), travel insurance, flight/train tickets, and hotel reservations.

Electronics:

1. **Mobile Phone & Charger**: Don't forget your mobile phone and charger, along with any other essential electronics like a camera, portable charger, headphones, and travel adapter.
2. **Travel Apps**: Download useful travel apps for navigation, currency conversion, language translation, and local recommendations.

Miscellaneous:

1. **Snacks**: Pack some snacks like granola bars, nuts, or dried fruits for quick energy during sightseeing or travel.
2. **Reusable Bag**: Carry a reusable shopping bag for groceries or souvenirs to reduce plastic waste.
3. **Guidebook/Maps**: Bring a guidebook or download offline maps to navigate the city and learn about attractions,

restaurants, and local customs.

Seasonal Items (Optional):

1. **Umbrella**: Consider packing a compact umbrella or raincoat if you're traveling during the rainy season.
2. **Swimsuit**: If your accommodation has a pool or you plan to visit thermal baths, pack a swimsuit.

Getting there and moving around.

Getting to Vienna, Austria, and moving around the city is relatively easy due to its well-developed transportation infrastructure. Here's a guide to help you navigate your journey:

Getting to Vienna:

1. **By Air**:
   - **Vienna International Airport (VIE)**: Vienna's main airport, VIE, is situated about 18 kilometers (11 miles) southeast of the city center. Travelers from all over the world can find it convenient because it provides a large number of domestic and international flights.
   - **Transportation from Airport**:
     - **Train**: The City Airport Train (CAT) and S-Bahn lines S7 connect the airport to the city center in approximately 15-25 minutes.
     - **Airport Shuttle/Bus**: Several airport shuttle services and buses operate between the airport and various locations in Vienna.
     - **Taxi/Car Rental**: Taxis and car rental services are available at the airport for travelers preferring a more direct and private transportation option.
2. **By Train**:

- **Vienna Central Station (Wien Hauptbahnhof)**: Vienna's main train station connects the city to various European destinations via high-speed trains (e.g., Railjet, EuroCity). The station offers domestic and international train services, making it a convenient option for travelers arriving by rail.

3. **By Bus**:
    - **International Buses**: Several international bus companies operate services to Vienna from major European cities, offering an affordable and comfortable travel option for budget-conscious travelers.

Moving Around Vienna:

1. **Public Transportation**:
    - **Vienna U-Bahn (Subway)**: The U-Bahn is Vienna's underground metro system, offering efficient and convenient transportation throughout the city. It operates from early morning until midnight (extended hours on weekends).
    - **Trams and Buses**: Vienna's extensive tram and bus network provides additional options for getting around the city, including access to areas not covered by the U-Bahn.
    - **Tickets and Passes**: Consider purchasing a Vienna Card or a public transport pass for unlimited travel on the U-Bahn, trams, and buses. Single tickets and multi-day passes are also available for purchase.

2. **Taxi and Ride-Sharing Services**:
    - **Taxis**: Taxis are readily available throughout Vienna and offer a convenient option for travelers seeking door-to-door transportation. Ensure the taxi meter is used, or agree on a fare before starting your journey.
    - **Ride-Sharing**: Services like Uber operate in Vienna, providing an alternative to traditional taxis with

upfront pricing and app-based booking.

3. **Biking**:
   - **City Bike**: Vienna offers a bike-sharing program called City Bike, allowing travelers to rent bikes from various stations throughout the city. Cycling is a popular and eco-friendly way to explore Vienna's attractions, parks, and scenic routes.

4. **Walking**:
   - **Pedestrian-Friendly**: Vienna's city center is pedestrian-friendly, making it easy to explore many attractions, historic sites, and cultural landmarks on foot. Enjoying the vivid ambiance, architecture, and street life of the city may be fully experienced by taking a stroll.

Practical Information

Language information

In Vienna, Austria, the official language spoken is German. However, you'll find that many people, especially those working in the tourism industry and younger generations, speak English fluently. Here's some language information to help you navigate your trip to Vienna:

German Language:

1. **Standard German (Hochdeutsch)**: This is the official and standard form of the German language spoken in Austria. It is taught in schools and used in formal settings, media, and written communication.
2. **Austrian German (Österreichisches Deutsch)**: While Standard German is understood and spoken in Austria, you'll also encounter variations of Austrian German in everyday conversations, regional dialects, and informal settings. Some words, phrases, or pronunciation may differ from Standard German.

Language Tips:

1. **Basic Phrases**: Learning a few basic German phrases can be helpful and appreciated by locals. Here are some useful phrases:
   - Hello: Hallo
   - Good morning: Guten Morgen
   - Good evening: Guten Abend
   - Please: Bitte
   - Thank you: Danke
   - Yes: Ja
   - No: Nein
   - Excuse me: Entschuldigung
   - Do you speak English?: Sprechen Sie Englisch?
2. **English Proficiency**: While many Austrians speak English, especially in tourist areas, it's courteous to start conversations with a polite greeting in German and ask if they speak English before proceeding. Most people will appreciate your effort to communicate in their language.
3. **Language Apps & Resources**: Consider downloading language apps like Duolingo, Babbel, or using language learning resources to familiarize yourself with basic German phrases and pronunciation before your trip.
4. **Signage & Information**: In Vienna, you'll find signs, menus, transportation information, and tourist attractions labeled in both German and English, making it easier for international travelers to navigate the city.

Cultural Considerations:

1. **Respect & Politeness**: Austrians value politeness, respect, and formalities in social interactions. Using formal greetings, addressing people by their titles (e.g., Herr for Mr., Frau for Mrs./Ms.), and showing courtesy in communication are appreciated cultural norms.
2. **Dialects & Regional Variations**: Be aware that Austria has

regional dialects and variations in language, especially in rural areas or smaller towns. While Standard German is widely understood, you may encounter local dialects or expressions that differ from standard pronunciation or vocabulary.

Currency and banking information

Currency and banking information is essential when traveling to Vienna, Austria, to ensure smooth financial transactions and money management. Here's an overview of the currency, banking services, and tips for handling money in Vienna:

Currency:

- **Euro (€)**: Austria uses the Euro as its official currency, denoted by the symbol "€" and the currency code EUR. The Euro is divided into 100 cents, with coins available in denominations of 1, 2, 5, 10, 20, and 50 cents, as well as 1 and 2 Euro coins. Banknotes come in denominations of 5, 10, 20, 50, 100, 200, and 500 Euros.

Banking and ATMs:

1. **Banking Hours**: Banks in Vienna generally operate from Monday to Friday, with standard business hours from 8:00 AM to 12:30 PM and 1:30 PM to 3:00 PM. Some branches may offer extended hours or Saturday morning services, but it's advisable to check specific bank hours in advance.
2. **ATMs (Automated Teller Machines)**:
   - **Availability**: ATMs are widely available throughout Vienna, including at airports, train stations, banks, shopping areas, and tourist areas.
   - **Currency Exchange**: ATMs offer the most favorable exchange rates for withdrawing Euros. Ensure your ATM card is enabled for international transactions, and

inform your bank of your travel dates to avoid any issues with withdrawals.

- **Fees**: Check with your bank regarding international ATM fees, currency conversion fees, and any additional charges for using ATMs abroad. Some ATMs may also charge a fee for withdrawals, so it's advisable to use ATMs affiliated with major banks or financial institutions.

3. **Credit and Debit Cards**:
   - **Acceptance**: In Vienna, many establishments including lodgings, dining options, retail stores, and tourist destinations accept major credit and debit cards, such as American Express, MasterCard, and Visa. Still, in smaller businesses or locations that might not take credit cards, always have some cash on hand.
   - **Chip and PIN**: European cards use a chip and PIN system for transactions. If your card does not have a chip and PIN, it may still work with a magnetic stripe and signature, but it's advisable to inform your bank and carry an alternative payment method if needed.
   - **Dynamic Currency Conversion**: Be cautious when using your card for transactions and avoid dynamic currency conversion (DCC) offers, as they may include unfavorable exchange rates and additional fees.

Currency Exchange:

- **Currency Exchange Offices**: Currency exchange offices (Wechselstuben) are available in Vienna for exchanging foreign currency into Euros. However, be cautious and compare exchange rates and fees, as some locations may offer less favorable rates or additional charges.
- **Hotels and Airports**: While hotels and airports offer currency exchange services, they often have higher fees and less favorable exchange rates compared to ATMs or banks. It's advisable to exchange a small amount for

immediate expenses and use ATMs for larger withdrawals or currency exchange needs.

Tips for Handling Money:

1. **Notify Your Bank**: Inform your bank of your travel dates, destination (Vienna, Austria), and notify them of any international transactions or ATM withdrawals to avoid potential issues with your account or card access.
2. **Carry Multiple Payment Methods**: Carry a combination of cash (Euros), credit/debit cards, and an alternative payment method (e.g., travel card) for flexibility and convenience.
3. **Safety and Security**: Be cautious when carrying cash, valuables, and personal belongings. Use secure ATMs located in well-lit and populated areas, keep an eye on your surroundings, and store money, cards, and travel documents in a secure location (e.g., hotel safe or money belt).

Safety information

Safety is essential when traveling to any destination, including Vienna, Austria. Here's some safety information and tips for travelers visiting Vienna:

General Safety Tips:

1. **Stay Informed**: Familiarize yourself with local laws, customs, and emergency contact information, including the nearest embassy or consulate for your country.
2. **Travel Insurance**: Purchase comprehensive travel insurance that covers medical emergencies, trip cancellations, and other unforeseen events during your

trip.

3. **Emergency Numbers**: Keep a list of emergency numbers, including local police, ambulance, fire department, and your country's embassy or consulate in Vienna.

Personal Safety:

1. **Awareness & Vigilance**: Maintain awareness of your surroundings, avoid poorly lit or unfamiliar areas at night, and be cautious in crowded places, tourist attractions, and public transportation.
2. **Secure Valuables**: Keep your belongings secure, including passports, cash, credit cards, and electronics. Use hotel safes, secure bags, and money belts to prevent theft or loss.
3. **Avoid Scams**: Be wary of common tourist scams, such as distraction techniques, fake petitions, counterfeit currency, and unsolicited offers or approaches from strangers.

Transportation Safety:

1. **Public Transportation**: Vienna has a reliable and safe public transportation system, including U-Bahn (subway), trams, and buses. Use reputable transportation services, purchase valid tickets, and be aware of your surroundings, especially during peak hours or late at night.
2. **Taxis and Ride-Sharing**: Use licensed taxis or reputable ride-sharing services like Uber. Ensure the taxi meter is used, agree on a fare before starting your journey, and avoid unlicensed or unmarked vehicles.

Health and Medical Safety:

1. **Medical Facilities**: Vienna has modern medical facilities, hospitals, and clinics offering quality healthcare services.

Carry a copy of your travel insurance, know the location of nearby medical facilities, and seek medical assistance if needed.

2. **Prescription Medications**: Pack any prescription medications in their original containers, carry a copy of your prescription.

Cultural and Social Etiquette:

1. **Respect Local Customs**: Be respectful of local customs, traditions, and cultural norms in Vienna. Dress appropriately, follow etiquette guidelines, and be mindful of religious, social, and cultural practices.

2. **Language & Communication**: While many Austrians speak English, learning basic German phrases, using polite greetings, and communicating respectfully can enhance your interactions with locals and minimize misunderstandings.

Natural Disasters and Weather:

1. **Weather Preparedness**: Vienna experiences a wide range of weather, so be ready for both mild summers and frigid winters as well as any probable weather-related events. For harsh weather or natural disasters, check the forecast, dress correctly, and adhere to safety precautions.

Chapter 2:
Must Visit Places in Vienna

Vienna, the capital of Austria, is a must-visit location for Germans and other Europeans because it provides a distinctive fusion of historical charm, cultural diversity, architectural beauty, and contemporary conveniences. Ten reasons to include Vienna on your vacation itinerary are as follows:

1. **Historical Landmarks**: Vienna is steeped in history, with magnificent landmarks like Schönbrunn Palace, Hofburg Imperial Palace, Belvedere Palace, and St. Stephen's Cathedral. Explore centuries-old architecture, royal residences, and UNESCO World Heritage Sites that showcase Vienna's rich cultural heritage.

2. **Cultural Capital**: Experience Vienna's vibrant cultural scene, including world-class museums, art galleries, theaters, and music venues. Attend classical concerts, opera performances, ballet shows, and cultural events that celebrate Vienna's contributions to music, art, and

literature.

3. **Musical Legacy**: Vienna is renowned as the "City of Music," with a storied musical legacy that includes famous composers like Mozart, Beethoven, Haydn, and Strauss. Visit iconic venues like the Vienna State Opera, Musikverein, and Haus der Musik to immerse yourself in classical music, operas, and concerts.

4. **Coffeehouse Culture**: Indulge in Vienna's legendary coffeehouse culture, where you can savor aromatic coffee, delicious pastries (like Sachertorte and Apfelstrudel), and immerse yourself in the city's literary and intellectual traditions. Experience the timeless elegance of Viennese coffeehouses, which are UNESCO Intangible Cultural Heritage sites.

5. **Culinary Delights**: Taste Vienna's diverse culinary scene, featuring traditional Austrian dishes, international cuisines, gourmet restaurants, street food markets, and wine taverns (Heuriger). Sample local specialties like Wiener Schnitzel, Tafelspitz, Kaiserschmarrn, and Austrian wines from the renowned vineyards surrounding Vienna.

6. **Green Spaces and Parks**: Explore Vienna's beautiful parks, gardens, and green spaces, such as the Vienna Woods (Wienerwald), Prater Park, Belvedere Gardens, and Burggarten. Enjoy leisurely strolls, picnics, cycling, hiking, and outdoor activities in these urban oases.

7. **Shopping and Fashion**: Shopaholics will love Vienna's diverse shopping districts, luxury boutiques, trendy fashion stores, artisan markets, and historic shopping arcades. Explore shopping streets like Mariahilfer Strasse, Graben, and Kohlmarkt for fashion, jewelry, souvenirs, and unique Viennese products.

8. **Festivals and Events**: Experience Vienna's vibrant festival scene, featuring annual events, cultural festivals, seasonal celebrations, and international gatherings. Attend events like the Vienna Festival, Vienna Pride, Christmas markets,

New Year's Eve concerts, and other festive occasions that showcase the city's lively spirit.

9. **Accessibility and Transportation**: Vienna's well-connected transportation network, including efficient public transportation (U-Bahn, trams, buses), bike-sharing programs, and pedestrian-friendly areas, makes it easy for visitors to explore the city's attractions, neighborhoods, and surrounding regions.

10. **Hospitality and Tourism**: Experience Austrian hospitality, friendly locals, welcoming atmosphere, and tourist-friendly amenities that cater to visitors from Germany, Europe, and around the world. Enjoy comfortable accommodations, excellent services, English-speaking staff, and personalized experiences that enhance your stay in Vienna.

These are the top destinations;

Schönbrunn Palace

It is located in the Hietzing district of Vienna, Austria, approximately 5 kilometers (3.1 miles) southwest of the city center. This magnificent Baroque palace complex is easily accessible by public transportation, including the U4 subway line (Schönbrunn station), trams, buses, and taxis.

Tourist Highlights:

1. **Grand Palace**: The centerpiece of Schönbrunn, the palace's stunning Baroque architecture, and lavish interiors offer a glimpse into Austria's imperial history. Visitors can explore the state rooms, imperial apartments, and ceremonial halls adorned with exquisite artworks, chandeliers, and historical furnishings.

2. **Gardens and Park**: The palace is surrounded by expansive gardens, landscaped parks, and intricate geometric

designs, featuring fountains, sculptures, flowerbeds, and walking paths. Highlights include the Great Parterre, Neptune Fountain, Gloriette, Palm House, and the Maze & Labyrinth.

3. **Zoo Vienna**: The Tiergarten Schönbrunn, located within the palace grounds, is the oldest zoo in the world, dating back to 1752. Visitors can explore diverse animal exhibits, endangered species, conservation programs, and family-friendly attractions.

4. **Privy Garden**: This hidden gem offers a serene escape from the crowds, featuring secluded pathways, manicured lawns, ornamental plants, and historic structures. The Privy Garden provides a tranquil setting for relaxation, photography, and enjoying the natural beauty of Schönbrunn.

5. **Marionette Theater**: Experience unique performances at the Marionette Theater, located near the palace gardens. This traditional puppet theater showcases classic operas, fairy tales, and theatrical productions, combining artistry, craftsmanship, and storytelling.

Hidden Gems:

1. **Orangery Garden**: Explore the Orangery Garden, featuring historic greenhouses, tropical plants, citrus trees, and seasonal displays. The Orangery Garden offers a peaceful retreat, stunning architecture, and hidden pathways for exploring the diverse plant collections.

2. **Wagenburg**: Visit the Wagenburg (Carriage Museum), located within the palace complex, featuring an impressive collection of historic carriages, royal vehicles, ceremonial coaches, and equestrian artifacts. The museum offers insights into transportation, craftsmanship, and Austrian royal history.

3. **Roman Ruins**: Discover the Roman Ruins, a hidden archaeological site within the palace gardens, featuring

ancient architectural remnants, archaeological excavations, and historical artifacts. The Roman Ruins provide a fascinating glimpse into Vienna's ancient past and cultural heritage.

4. **Cafés and Restaurants**: Enjoy traditional Viennese cuisine, coffee, and pastries at the palace's cafés, restaurants, and outdoor terraces. Experience dining with panoramic views of the gardens, palace, and surrounding landmarks while savoring local flavors and culinary delights.

Hofburg Palace

The Hofburg Palace is centrally located in the heart of Vienna, Austria's capital city. The palace complex occupies a significant portion of the Innere Stadt (Inner City) district, and its expansive grounds encompass various buildings, courtyards, and squares that reflect centuries of imperial history and architectural evolution.

Tourist Highlights:

1. **Imperial Apartments**: Explore the lavishly decorated rooms, chambers, and private apartments that once housed the Habsburg emperors and empresses, showcasing opulent furnishings, artwork, and historical artifacts.

2. **Sisi Museum**: Visit the Sisi Museum, dedicated to Empress Elisabeth of Austria ("Sisi"), featuring personal belongings, portraits, dresses, and insights into her life, legacy, and enduring fascination with the public.

3. **Silver Collection**: Admire the exquisite tableware, porcelain, glassware, and ceremonial objects displayed in the Silver Collection, showcasing the grandeur and luxury of imperial banquets and festivities.

4. **Spanish Riding School**: Experience the elegance of the world-famous Lipizzaner horses performing classical

dressage routines, training sessions, and special performances in the historic setting of the Spanish Riding School within the Hofburg complex.

5. **Treasury (Schatzkammer)**: Discover the Treasury's priceless collection of imperial regalia, crowns, jewels, religious artifacts, and treasures that highlight Austria's royal history, power, and influence.

Hidden Gems:

1. **Augustinian Wing & Augustinian Church**: Explore the Augustinian Wing, home to the Augustinian Church, where many Habsburg weddings, funerals, and religious ceremonies took place. Admire the Baroque architecture, frescoes, altarpieces, and the tomb of Emperor Franz Joseph I and Empress Elisabeth in the church's crypt.

2. **Hofburg Crypt**: Descend into the Hofburg Crypt beneath the Capuchin Church, where members of the Habsburg dynasty are entombed in elaborate sarcophagi, crypts, and vaults, offering a fascinating glimpse into Austria's imperial history, traditions, and funerary practices.

3. **Heldenplatz & Volksgarten**: Wander through Heldenplatz (Heroes' Square) and Volksgarten (People's Garden), adjacent to the Hofburg Palace, offering tranquil green spaces, historic monuments, statues, and scenic views of the palace, gardens, and surrounding landmarks.

4. **Burggarten & Palm House**: Relax in the Burggarten (Castle Garden), featuring landscaped gardens, monuments, and the historic Palm House, a beautiful glasshouse showcasing tropical plants, exotic flowers, and a serene oasis in the heart of Vienna.

5. **Alte Hofburg**: Discover the Alte Hofburg (Old Hofburg), the medieval core of the palace complex, featuring historic buildings, courtyards, and remnants of the original medieval palace that provide insights into Vienna's early history, architecture, and urban development.

St. Stephen's Cathedral

St. Stephen's Cathedral, commonly known as Stephansdom, is located in the heart of Vienna's historic center, surrounded by the bustling pedestrian zones and vibrant streets of the city. Here's a description of its location, tourist highlights, and hidden gems:

Location:

St. Stephen's Cathedral is situated in Stephansplatz, a central square in Vienna's 1st district (Innere Stadt). The cathedral's iconic Gothic spire dominates the skyline, making it a recognizable landmark amidst the city's historic architecture, shopping streets, cafes, and cultural attractions.

Tourist Highlights:

1. **Gothic Architecture**: Admire the stunning Gothic architecture, intricate details, and ornate design elements of St. Stephen's Cathedral, including its iconic multicolored tile roof, towers, and facades.
2. **South Tower (Südturm)**: Climb the 343-step spiral staircase to the South Tower for panoramic views of Vienna's skyline, historic center, and surrounding landmarks from the viewing platform.
3. **Catacombs and Treasury**: Explore the cathedral's catacombs, where you can visit the tombs, crypts, and burial chambers of prominent historical figures, as well as the Treasury featuring religious artifacts, relics, and treasures.
4. **High Altar and Interior**: Marvel at the cathedral's interior, including the High Altar, pulpit, stained glass windows, frescoes, sculptures, and religious artworks that showcase centuries of craftsmanship, artistry, and religious devotion.

Hidden Gems:

1. **Roof Tours**: Join a guided roof tour or explore the cathedral's rooftop terraces to get a unique perspective on its architecture, decorative details, and panoramic views of Vienna.
2. **Mozart's Wedding**: Discover the historical legend of Mozart's Wedding, commemorated by a plaque near the main entrance, where Wolfgang Amadeus Mozart and Constanze Weber were married in 1782.
3. **Pummerin Bell**: Learn about the cathedral's famous bell, the Pummerin, one of the largest bells in Europe, and its history, significance, and cultural importance to Vienna.
4. **Organ Concerts**: Attend an organ concert or musical performance at St. Stephen's Cathedral to experience its acoustics, ambiance, and spiritual resonance in a live music setting.
5. **Hidden Chapels and Altars**: Explore the cathedral's chapels, altars, and side aisles to discover hidden gems, religious artworks, statues, and sacred spaces dedicated to saints, religious orders, and historical events.
6. **Vienna Mass**: Attend a Vienna Mass, liturgical service, or religious ceremony at St. Stephen's Cathedral to experience its spiritual significance, architectural grandeur, and cultural heritage as the mother church of the Archdiocese of Vienna.

Belvedere Palace

Belvedere Palace is located in the heart of Vienna, Austria, within the historic Landstraße district. It is easily accessible by public transportation, including trams, buses, and the U-Bahn (subway), making it a convenient destination for visitors exploring Vienna.

Tourist Highlights:

1. **Upper Belvedere**: This magnificent Baroque palace complex consists of two main buildings, the Upper

Belvedere and Lower Belvedere, surrounded by beautiful gardens, fountains, and sculptures.

2. **Art Collections**: The Upper Belvedere houses an impressive collection of Austrian art from the Middle Ages to the present day, including iconic masterpieces by Gustav Klimt, Egon Schiele, and other renowned artists. Visitors can admire famous works like "The Kiss" and "Judith" by Klimt, along with numerous paintings, sculptures, and decorative arts.

3. **Palace Interiors**: Explore the lavish interiors of the palace, featuring grand halls, staterooms, royal apartments, and Baroque architecture that reflects the opulence and grandeur of the Habsburg dynasty.

4. **Gardens and Grounds**: Wander through the meticulously landscaped gardens, terraces, and pathways surrounding the palace complex, offering scenic views, photo opportunities, and a peaceful retreat from the bustling city.

Hidden Gems:

1. **Lower Belvedere and Orangery**: While the Upper Belvedere is a popular tourist attraction, don't overlook the Lower Belvedere and Orangery, which feature additional art exhibitions, temporary displays, and events that showcase Vienna's cultural heritage.

2. **Belvedere 21 (21er Haus)**: Located near the main Belvedere Palace complex, Belvedere 21 is a contemporary art museum housed in a striking modernist building. Explore exhibitions, installations, and innovative artworks by contemporary artists, offering a contrast to the historic collections at the main Belvedere Palace.

3. **Klimt's Beethoven Frieze**: Admire Gustav Klimt's monumental Beethoven Frieze, located in a dedicated exhibition space within the Upper Belvedere. This iconic work of art, inspired by Beethoven's Ninth Symphony, showcases Klimt's distinctive style, symbolism, and artistic

vision.

4. **Café and Gift Shop**: Relax and unwind at the palace's café, offering panoramic views of the gardens, sculptures, and surrounding landmarks. Don't forget to visit the gift shop, where you can purchase souvenirs, art prints, books, and unique gifts inspired by the Belvedere Palace and its collections

The Vienna State Opera

The Vienna State Opera (Wiener Staatsoper) is one of the most prestigious opera houses in the world, located in the heart of Vienna, Austria. Here's a description of its location, tourist highlights, and hidden gems:

Location:

The Vienna State Opera is situated in the Innere Stadt district, Vienna's historic city center, on the famous Ringstrasse boulevard. Its exact address is Opernring 2, 1010 Vienna, Austria. The opera house is easily accessible by public transportation, including the U-Bahn (subway), trams, buses, and is within walking distance of many attractions, hotels, restaurants, and shopping areas in Vienna.

Tourist Highlights:

1. **Architectural Beauty**: Admire the stunning Neo-Renaissance architecture of the Vienna State Opera, designed by renowned architects August Sicard von Sicardsburg and Eduard van der Null. The grand facade, majestic staircase, and intricate details showcase the opulence and elegance of the imperial era.
2. **Opera Performances**: Experience world-class opera, ballet, concerts, and performances at the Vienna State Opera. Attend a live performance to witness talented artists,

renowned conductors, and exquisite productions in one of the world's leading opera houses.

3. **Guided Tours**: Take a guided tour of the Vienna State Opera to explore its magnificent interiors, history, backstage areas, and learn about its prestigious legacy, famous artists, and cultural significance. Tours offer insights into the opera house's architecture, acoustics, productions, and behind-the-scenes operations.

4. **Vienna Opera Ball**: Attend the annual Vienna Opera Ball, a prestigious event featuring elegant gowns, traditional waltzes, live music, and a glamorous atmosphere. Experience this iconic cultural event that attracts celebrities, dignitaries, and opera enthusiasts from around the world.

Hidden Gems:

1. **Standing Room Tickets**: Experience opera performances on a budget by purchasing standing room tickets (Stehplätze) at the Vienna State Opera. Enjoy a unique perspective, acoustics, and atmosphere from various standing areas within the opera house, offering an affordable way to enjoy world-class performances.

2. **Vienna Opera Live Streams**: Watch live streams of Vienna State Opera performances at the Opera House's outdoor screen (Staatsoper für alle) or nearby locations like Karajan Platz or Herbert von Karajan Platz. Experience the magic of opera for free with fellow music lovers, tourists, and locals in a vibrant outdoor setting.

3. **Vienna State Opera Museum**: Visit the Vienna State Opera Museum (Haus der Wiener Staatsoper) located inside the opera house, showcasing a fascinating collection of costumes, props, photographs, memorabilia, and artifacts from its storied history. Explore exhibits, archives, and learn about the opera house's evolution, artists, productions, and cultural impact.

4. **Vienna State Opera Shop**: Discover unique souvenirs, gifts, merchandise, and opera-related items at the Vienna State Opera Shop (Staatsopern-Shop), located inside the opera house. Shop for CDs, DVDs, books, posters, memorabilia, and exclusive products featuring renowned artists, performances, and iconic designs from the Vienna State Opera.

The Albertina Museum

The Albertina Museum is located in the heart of Vienna, Austria, near the Vienna State Opera and the Hofburg Palace. This prestigious art museum is situated in the historic center of Vienna, making it easily accessible and a must-visit attraction for art enthusiasts, culture lovers, and tourists alike.

Tourist Highlights:

1. **Impressive Art Collection**: The Albertina Museum houses an extensive collection of artworks, featuring prints, drawings, watercolors, photographs, and paintings by renowned artists such as Albrecht Dürer, Michelangelo, Raphael, Rembrandt, Monet, Picasso, and Klimt.
2. **State Rooms and Architecture**: Explore the museum's elegant state rooms, Baroque architecture, and historic interiors, offering a glimpse into Vienna's imperial past, royal residences, and cultural heritage.
3. **Temporary Exhibitions**: The Albertina hosts temporary exhibitions, showcasing contemporary art, special collections, thematic exhibitions, and rotating displays that highlight diverse artistic styles, movements, and periods.
4. **Palais Garden**: Enjoy the museum's picturesque Palais Garden, a tranquil oasis in the heart of Vienna, featuring sculptures, fountains, manicured lawns, and scenic views of the city skyline.
5. **Albertina Modern**: Visit Albertina Modern, the museum's

contemporary art extension located near the Vienna State Opera, featuring modern and contemporary artworks, exhibitions, and innovative installations by contemporary artists.

Hidden Gems:

1. **Graphic Arts Collection**: Delve deeper into the museum's graphic arts collection, featuring a vast array of prints, drawings, and illustrations that span various artistic movements, techniques, and periods, offering insights into the evolution of printmaking and drawing practices.
2. **Photographic Collection**: Explore the Albertina's extensive photographic collection, showcasing historical and contemporary photography, iconic images, experimental works, and thematic exhibitions that highlight the art of photography and its impact on visual culture.
3. **Architectural Drawings**: Discover the museum's collection of architectural drawings, sketches, and designs, featuring plans, blueprints, and models that document Vienna's architectural history, urban development, and iconic landmarks.
4. **Educational Programs and Workshops**: Participate in educational programs, workshops, guided tours, and interactive experiences offered by the Albertina, providing opportunities to engage with artworks, artists, curators, and fellow visitors in meaningful ways.
5. **Café and Restaurant**: Relax and unwind at the museum's café and restaurant, offering gourmet cuisine, Viennese specialties, panoramic views of the Palais Garden, and a tranquil setting to enjoy a meal, coffee, or afternoon tea amidst the museum's historic ambiance.

Vienna Prater:

Vienna Prater, commonly referred to as "Prater," is a large public park in Vienna, Austria, known for its iconic Ferris wheel, amusement park, green spaces, and recreational activities. Located in Leopoldstadt, the second district of Vienna, the Prater is easily accessible by public transportation and attracts both locals and tourists seeking entertainment, relaxation, and outdoor adventures.

Tourist Highlights:

1. **Giant Ferris Wheel (Riesenrad)**: One of Vienna's most recognizable landmarks, the Giant Ferris Wheel offers panoramic views of the city skyline, Danube River, and surrounding areas. Dating back to 1897, this historic attraction features traditional wooden cabins and modern gondolas, providing visitors with a unique perspective of Vienna.

2. **Amusement Park**: Explore the Prater's amusement park area, featuring a variety of rides, attractions, games, and entertainment options for visitors of all ages. From classic carousels and roller coasters to thrill rides and family-friendly activities, the Prater offers fun-filled experiences and nostalgic charm.

3. **Green Spaces**: Enjoy leisurely strolls, picnics, and outdoor activities in the Prater's expansive green spaces, parks, and recreational areas. The park's lush landscapes, walking paths, and scenic views provide a tranquil escape from the bustling city center.

4. **Prater Hauptallee**: Walk, jog, or cycle along the Prater Hauptallee, a historic avenue lined with trees, statues, and landmarks. This iconic boulevard connects the entrance of the Prater to the Lusthaus, offering a picturesque route for outdoor enthusiasts and nature lovers.

5. **Prater Liliputbahn**: Ride the Prater Liliputbahn, a charming miniature railway that travels through the park, providing scenic views, historical insights, and a unique perspective of the Prater's attractions, landscapes, and

hidden gems.

Hidden Gems:

1. **Wurstelprater**: Discover the nostalgic charm of Wurstelprater, Vienna's oldest amusement park, featuring classic rides, attractions, games, and entertainment. This historic section of the Prater offers a blend of vintage attractions, cultural experiences, and family-friendly fun that captures the essence of traditional Austrian amusement parks.

2. **Kunsthalle Wien**: Visit Kunsthalle Wien, a contemporary art space located near the Prater, featuring exhibitions, installations, and events showcasing local and international artists. Explore the museum's innovative programming, modern architecture, and cultural initiatives that enrich Vienna's vibrant arts scene.

3. **Vienna Prater Biergarten**: Experience Vienna's beer culture at the Vienna Prater Biergarten, a traditional beer garden offering local brews, Austrian cuisine, live music, and outdoor seating. Relax, socialize, and enjoy authentic flavors, regional specialties, and seasonal dishes in a relaxed and festive atmosphere.

4. **Hochstrahlbrunnen**: Admire the Hochstrahlbrunnen, a historic fountain located in the Prater, featuring an illuminated water display, statues, and ornate architecture. This iconic landmark serves as a gathering place, photo opportunity, and cultural symbol within the park.

5. **Prater Museum**: Explore the Prater Museum, a hidden gem dedicated to the history, heritage, and evolution of the Prater amusement park, rides, attractions, and cultural significance. Discover artifacts, photographs, memorabilia, and interactive exhibits that chronicle the Prater's fascinating past and enduring legacy.

The Vienna Woods

The Vienna Woods, known as the "Wienerwald" in German, is a picturesque forested area located to the west of Vienna, Austria's capital city. This expansive natural region encompasses a diverse landscape of rolling hills, dense forests, charming villages, vineyards, and historical landmarks. Here's a description of the Vienna Woods, highlighting tourist attractions and hidden gems:

Tourist Highlights:

1. **Lainzer Tiergarten**: This wildlife preserve offers hiking trails, scenic viewpoints, and the former imperial hunting grounds of Emperor Franz Joseph. Visitors can explore the park, observe local wildlife, and enjoy panoramic views of Vienna.
2. **Mayerling**: Visit the historic site of Mayerling, the former hunting lodge and tragic location of the Mayerling Incident involving Crown Prince Rudolf. Explore the memorial chapel, museum, and learn about the fascinating history of this royal site.
3. **Heiligenkreuz Abbey**: Discover Austria's oldest Cistercian monastery, Heiligenkreuz Abbey, known for its Gothic architecture, historic library, Gregorian chants, and tranquil surroundings. Explore the abbey church, cloisters, and beautiful landscaped gardens.
4. **Klosterneuburg Monastery**: Explore this stunning monastery complex, featuring a beautiful church, museum, winery, and medieval cloisters. Admire the artistic treasures, Baroque architecture, and learn about the monastery's rich history and cultural significance.
5. **Vienna Woods Railway (Wienerwald-Bahn)**: Enjoy a scenic train ride through the Vienna Woods, connecting Vienna with charming towns like Baden, Mödling, and other picturesque destinations. Experience the beauty of the landscape, vineyards, and historical landmarks along

the railway route.

6. **Wine Taverns (Heuriger)**: Experience the traditional Austrian wine culture by visiting local wine taverns (Heuriger) in the Vienna Woods. Enjoy regional wines, Austrian cuisine, live music, and a cozy atmosphere in these charming establishments.

Hidden Gems:

1. **Hiking and Cycling Trails**: Explore hidden trails, hiking paths, and cycling routes throughout the Vienna Woods, offering scenic views, natural beauty, and opportunities for outdoor activities. Discover lesser-known trails, tranquil spots, and hidden gems away from the main tourist areas.

2. **Vineyards and Wine Cellars**: Venture off the beaten path to discover hidden vineyards, wine cellars, and boutique wineries in the Vienna Woods region. Experience wine tastings, vineyard tours, and learn about local grape varieties, winemaking traditions, and Austrian viticulture.

3. **Local Villages and Towns**: Explore charming villages, historic towns, and hidden gems in the Vienna Woods region, such as Baden, Mödling, Perchtoldsdorf, and other picturesque destinations. Discover local culture, traditions, artisanal products, and immerse yourself in the authentic Austrian countryside.

4. **Natural Springs and Wellness**: Visit natural springs, mineral baths, and wellness centers in the Vienna Woods region, offering relaxation, rejuvenation, and therapeutic treatments. Experience spa resorts, thermal baths, and wellness retreats nestled within the tranquil surroundings of the Vienna Woods.

5. **Historical Sites and Landmarks**: Discover hidden historical sites, ruins, and landmarks scattered throughout the Vienna Woods, including medieval castles, ancient ruins, and archaeological sites. Explore lesser-known

attractions, historical monuments, and cultural heritage sites off the beaten path.

The Kunsthistorisches Museum

The Kunsthistorisches Museum (Museum of Art History) is located in Vienna, Austria, on the famous Ringstrasse boulevard, known for its prestigious collection of fine arts, historical treasures, and architectural beauty. Here's a description of the location, tourist highlights, and hidden gems of the Kunsthistorisches Museum:

Location:

- **Accessibility**: The museum is centrally located in Vienna's historic city center, easily accessible by public transportation (U-Bahn, tram, bus) and within walking distance of other landmarks, attractions, and cultural institutions.

Tourist Highlights:

1. **Impressive Architecture**: Admire the museum's stunning Neo-Renaissance architecture, grand staircase, dome, and decorative facade, designed by renowned architects Gottfried Semper and Karl von Hasenauer.
2. **Art Collections**: Explore the museum's extensive collection of European art, featuring masterpieces by renowned artists such as Raphael, Vermeer, Rembrandt, Caravaggio, Titian, and Pieter Bruegel the Elder.
3. **Egyptian and Near Eastern Collection**: Discover ancient artifacts, sculptures, mummies, and treasures from ancient Egypt, the Near East, and the Mediterranean region, showcasing the museum's diverse archaeological collections.
4. **Kunstkammer Vienna**: Experience the museum's

Kunstkammer (Chamber of Art and Wonders), featuring a unique collection of Renaissance and Baroque artworks, curiosities, scientific instruments, and precious objects from the Habsburg dynasty.

Hidden Gems:

1. **Coin Collection**: Visit the Numismatic Collection, housing one of the world's largest and most comprehensive collections of coins, medals, and monetary artifacts, spanning ancient times to the present day.
2. **Sculpture Garden**: Explore the museum's sculpture garden and outdoor spaces, featuring monumental sculptures, fountains, and architectural elements that provide a tranquil oasis in the heart of Vienna.
3. **Special Exhibitions**: Check the museum's calendar for temporary exhibitions, special installations, curated displays, and events that offer unique insights into specific artists, periods, themes, or collections.
4. **Guided Tours and Workshops**: Participate in guided tours, workshops, lectures, or educational programs offered by the museum, providing in-depth insights, expert commentary, and interactive experiences for visitors of all ages.
5. **Museum Café and Shop**: Relax and unwind at the museum's café, enjoy Viennese coffee, pastries, or light refreshments in a beautiful setting. Explore the museum shop for unique gifts, souvenirs, art books, and exclusive merchandise inspired by the museum's collections and exhibitions.

Rathaus (Vienna City Hall)

It is located in the heart of Vienna, Austria's capital city, within the historic Innere Stadt (Inner City) district. Situated on the famous Rathausplatz, the Rathaus is a prominent Neo-Gothic-style building that serves as the seat of the city government and a symbol of Vienna's rich history and cultural heritage.

Tourist Highlights:

1. **Neo-Gothic Architecture**: Admire the stunning Neo-Gothic architecture of the Rathaus, featuring intricate details, spires, arcades, and a magnificent facade that showcases Vienna's architectural grandeur.
2. **Rathausplatz Events**: Experience seasonal events, festivals, markets, and cultural celebrations held at Rathausplatz, such as the Vienna Christmas Market, Film Festival, and numerous concerts, exhibitions, and public gatherings.
3. **Rathauspark**: Explore the beautiful Rathauspark surrounding the City Hall, featuring landscaped gardens, statues, fountains, and green spaces where locals and tourists can relax, picnic, or enjoy leisurely strolls.
4. **Guided Tours**: Take a guided tour of the Rathaus to explore the interior, council chambers, historic rooms, and learn about Vienna's local government, history, and cultural significance from knowledgeable guides.
5. **View from Rathaus Tower**: Climb the Rathaus Tower for panoramic views of Vienna, offering stunning vistas of the city skyline, landmarks, and surrounding areas from a unique vantage point.

Hidden Gems:

1. **Vienna City Hall Clock Tower**: Discover the intricate details and craftsmanship of the Rathaus Clock Tower, featuring ornate designs, statues, and a historic clock mechanism that has been a landmark of Vienna for centuries.
2. **Historic Courtyard**: Explore the hidden courtyards, arcades, and inner passages of the Rathaus, showcasing architectural details, sculptures, and historic elements that

reflect Vienna's rich history and cultural heritage.

3. **City Council Chambers**: Visit the City Council Chambers inside the Rathaus, featuring impressive architecture, artworks, and historical artifacts that showcase Vienna's political history, governance, and cultural significance.

4. **Cultural Events and Exhibitions**: Attend special events, exhibitions, and cultural programs held at the Rathaus, such as art installations, performances, lectures, and community gatherings that highlight Vienna's vibrant arts and cultural scene.

5. **Rathaus Cellars**: Explore the Rathaus Cellars, a hidden gem beneath the City Hall, featuring historic vaulted chambers, wine cellars, and tasting rooms where you can sample Austrian wines, attend wine events, or explore the underground architecture and history of the Rathaus.

Karlskirche (St. Charles's Church)

It is located in Vienna, Austria, in the district of Wieden, near the Karlsplatz. It stands as one of Vienna's most iconic Baroque landmarks, known for its stunning architecture, rich history, and cultural significance.

Tourist Highlights:

1. **Architectural Grandeur**: Karlskirche is renowned for its impressive Baroque architecture, featuring a majestic dome, columns, sculptures, and intricate detailing designed by the famous architect Johann Bernhard Fischer von Erlach.

2. **Dome and Frescoes**: The church's dome is adorned with breathtaking frescoes by Johann Michael Rottmayr, depicting scenes from the life of St. Charles Borromeo, the church's namesake.

3. **High Altar**: The High Altar inside Karlskirche is adorned with an impressive painting of the "Glory of St. Charles,"

sculptures, and decorative elements that showcase Baroque artistry and religious symbolism.

4. **Panoramic Views**: Visitors can ascend the dome's viewing platform for panoramic views of Vienna, offering a unique perspective of the city's skyline, landmarks, and surrounding areas.

5. **Religious Services and Events**: Karlskirche serves as an active parish church, hosting religious services, concerts, choir performances, and special events throughout the year, showcasing Vienna's musical heritage and cultural traditions.

Hidden Gems:

1. **Tomb of St. Charles Borromeo**: Inside Karlskirche, visitors can view the tomb of St. Charles Borromeo, the church's patron saint, and explore the chapel dedicated to his life, miracles, and religious contributions.

2. **Pillar Veneration**: The church features a Vow Pillar (or Plague Column) outside, where visitors and locals traditionally come to pray, make offerings, and seek blessings, reflecting the church's historical significance during the plague epidemic.

3. **Karlsplatz and Gardens**: Surrounding Karlskirche, visitors can explore Karlsplatz, a bustling square featuring gardens, fountains, pathways, and outdoor spaces for relaxation, events, and gatherings. The square often hosts cultural events, festivals, markets, and performances that showcase Vienna's vibrant atmosphere.

4. **Karlskirche Museum**: Adjacent to the church, visitors can explore the Karlskirche Museum, featuring exhibits, artifacts, historical information, and multimedia presentations that provide insights into the church's construction, architecture, religious significance, and cultural impact.

5. **Cultural Events and Concerts**: Karlskirche is renowned for

its acoustics, making it a popular venue for classical concerts, choir performances, and cultural events. Visitors can attend musical performances, recitals, and special events that showcase Vienna's rich musical heritage and artistic traditions within the church's magnificent setting.

The Spanish Riding School

The Spanish Riding School (Spanische Hofreitschule) is located in the heart of Vienna, Austria, within the Hofburg Palace complex, specifically in the historic center known as the Inner City (Innere Stadt). Here's a description highlighting its location, tourist highlights, and hidden gems:

Location:

- **Neighborhood**: The Spanish Riding School is situated in the historic center of Vienna, surrounded by iconic landmarks, attractions, shopping districts, restaurants, and cultural institutions.

Tourist Highlights:

1. **Hofburg Palace**: The Spanish Riding School is part of the Hofburg Palace complex, Vienna's former imperial residence, featuring museums, Imperial Apartments, Silver Collection, Sisi Museum, and the Imperial Chapel (Burgkapelle).
2. **Michaelerplatz**: Adjacent to the Spanish Riding School, Michaelerplatz is a bustling square featuring the Michaelertrakt (Michael Wing) of the Hofburg Palace, archaeological excavations, historic architecture, and the Looshaus designed by Adolf Loos.
3. **St. Michael's Church (Michaelerkirche)**: Located near Michaelerplatz, this beautiful Baroque church features stunning architecture, a historic crypt, and unique

artworks, including the Beethoven Memorial.

4. **Kohlmarkt and Graben**: These prestigious shopping streets are a short walk from the Spanish Riding School, featuring luxury boutiques, international brands, historic architecture, elegant storefronts, cafes, and restaurants.

5. **Albertina Museum**: A few minutes' walk from the Spanish Riding School, the Albertina Museum showcases an impressive collection of prints, drawings, photography, and temporary exhibitions, including works by renowned artists like Monet, Picasso, and Dürer.

Hidden Gems:

1. **Spanish Riding School Morning Exercise**: Attend the morning exercise sessions (Morgenarbeit) to watch the Lipizzaner horses training, performing dressage routines, and practicing classical techniques in the stunning Winter Riding School arena.

2. **Hofburg Palace Imperial Apartments**: Explore the Imperial Apartments and Sisi Museum to learn about the lives, history, and legacy of the Habsburg dynasty, Empress Elisabeth (Sisi), and the imperial family.

3. **Augustinerkirche (Augustinian Church)**: Visit this historic church near the Spanish Riding School, featuring Baroque architecture, the Habsburg family crypt, stunning frescoes, and the Canova's Monument to Maria Christina of Austria.

4. **Bermuda Triangle (Bermudadreieck)**: Explore this vibrant nightlife area near the Spanish Riding School, featuring bars, pubs, cafes, live music venues, and a lively atmosphere popular with locals and visitors alike.

5. **Imperial Crypt (Kapuzinergruft)**: Discover the Habsburgs' final resting place in the Kapuzinerkirche crypt, featuring tombs, sarcophagi, memorials, and the Ducal Crypt for other members of the imperial family.

The Haus der Musik

The Haus der Musik, or House of Music, is located in the heart of Vienna, Austria, in the Innere Stadt (Inner City) district. Specifically, it is situated on Seilerstätte 30, near the famous St. Stephen's Cathedral (Stephansdom) and the Vienna State Opera. The address places it within the historic and culturally rich city center, making it easily accessible for tourists exploring Vienna's top attractions.

Tourist Highlights Nearby:

1. **St. Stephen's Cathedral (Stephansdom)**: One of Vienna's most iconic landmarks, this Gothic cathedral features stunning architecture, including the South Tower with panoramic views of the city.
2. **Vienna State Opera**: A renowned opera house showcasing world-class performances and classical music. Its architecture is an attraction in itself, and visitors can enjoy both guided tours and live performances.
3. **Albertina Museum**: Located in the vicinity, this art museum housed in a former palace displays an extensive collection of prints, drawings, and photography, including works by renowned artists.
4. **Hofburg Palace**: A historic imperial palace complex that houses museums, the Spanish Riding School, and the Imperial Apartments, offering a glimpse into Vienna's royal history.
5. **Graben and Kohlmarkt**: These bustling shopping streets are lined with luxury boutiques, international brands, and elegant storefronts, making them popular among shoppers and visitors.
6. **MuseumsQuartier (MQ)**: Vienna's cultural district, hosting various museums, art galleries, and creative

spaces, providing a vibrant atmosphere for art enthusiasts.

Hidden Gems in the Vicinity:

1. **Mozarthaus Vienna**: Explore the former residence of Wolfgang Amadeus Mozart, offering insights into the life and work of the legendary composer.
2. **Peterskirche (St. Peter's Church)**: A beautiful Baroque church known for its impressive interior, including frescoes and intricate design.
3. **Minoritenkirche (Minorite Church)**: This Gothic church features a stunning facade and interior, offering a peaceful retreat from the bustling city.
4. **Plague Column (Pestsäule)**: Located on Graben, this Baroque column commemorates the city's survival of the plague and is a notable piece of public art.
5. **Judenplatz (Jewish Square)**: Discover this historic square with the Holocaust Memorial and the Museum Judenplatz, dedicated to Vienna's Jewish history.
6. **Vienna City Park (Stadtpark)**: A tranquil park with beautiful greenery, notable monuments, and the famous statue of Johann Strauss II, offering a relaxing escape.
7. **Teinfaltstraße and Blutgasse**: Wander through these charming narrow streets filled with historic buildings, cafes, and a glimpse of traditional Viennese life.
8. **Karlsplatz**: A central square with cultural institutions, including the Karlskirche, Vienna's iconic Baroque church.

MuseumsQuartier (MQ)

MuseumsQuartier (MQ) is one of the largest cultural quarters in the world, located in the heart of Vienna's city center. Here's a detailed description highlighting tourist attractions and hidden gems within the MuseumsQuartier:

Tourist Highlights:

1. **Museums and Institutions**:
   - **Leopold Museum**: Known for its extensive collection of Austrian art, including works by Egon Schiele and Gustav Klimt.
   - **Museum of Modern Art (mumok)**: Features a vast collection of modern and contemporary art, including works by Andy Warhol, Pablo Picasso, and Roy Lichtenstein.
   - **Kunsthalle Wien**: Offers exhibitions of contemporary art, installations, and multimedia projects.
   - **Architekturzentrum Wien (Az W)**: Focuses on architecture, urban planning, and design through exhibitions, lectures, and events.
2. **Courtyard and Outdoor Spaces**:
   - **MQ Courtyards**: The expansive courtyards of MQ serve as a vibrant social hub, offering outdoor seating, cafes, art installations, events, and a relaxed atmosphere for visitors to enjoy.
3. **Cafes and Restaurants**:
   - **Café Leopold**: A trendy cafe located in the heart of MQ, offering a stylish ambiance, outdoor seating, contemporary cuisine, and a lively atmosphere.
   - **MQ Daily**: A popular cafe and bistro serving fresh coffee, breakfast, lunch, snacks, and drinks in a relaxed setting.
4. **Events and Festivals**:
   - **Vienna Fashion Week**: Held annually at MQ, featuring fashion shows, designer showcases, exhibitions, and events celebrating Austrian and international fashion.
   - **Summer Night Concert**: Experience open-air concerts, performances, film screenings, festivals, and cultural events held in the courtyards and outdoor spaces of MQ.

Hidden Gems:

1. **ZOOM Children's Museum**: A hidden gem within MQ, offering interactive exhibits, workshops, and activities designed for children and families to explore art, culture, and creativity together.
2. **Dschungel Wien**: Located within MQ, Dschungel Wien is a theater specializing in performances for children and young audiences, offering a diverse program of plays, dance, music, and puppetry.
3. **Tanzquartier Wien**: A contemporary dance center located within MQ, featuring performances, workshops, residencies, and events showcasing innovative dance artists, choreographers, and companies from Austria and around the world.
4. **Q21 Artist-in-Residence Studios**: Explore the Q21 Artist-in-Residence studios, a creative hub for artists, designers, and cultural practitioners from various disciplines to live, work, collaborate, and showcase their talents within MQ.
5. **Hidden Courtyards and Art Installations**: Wander through the hidden courtyards, alleyways, and outdoor spaces of MQ to discover unique art installations, sculptures, murals, and creative expressions by local and international artists.

Hundertwasserhaus:

Location: Hundertwasserhaus is located in the Landstraße district of Vienna, Austria. Specifically, it can be found at Kegelgasse 34-38, 1030 Vienna.

Tourist Highlights:

1. **Architectural Marvel**: Designed by the renowned Austrian artist Friedensreich Hundertwasser, the Hundertwasserhaus is a unique architectural masterpiece characterized by its vibrant colors, irregular shapes, undulating floors, and tree tenants (trees integrated into

the building's design).

2. **Public Housing Project**: The Hundertwasserhaus is not just an artistic landmark but also serves as a public housing project, providing residents with a creative and eco-friendly living environment designed to harmonize with nature.

3. **Gift Shop & Museum**: Adjacent to the Hundertwasserhaus, visitors can explore the Kunst Haus Wien, a museum and gift shop dedicated to Hundertwasser's works, showcasing exhibitions, artworks, and merchandise related to the artist's life and creative vision.

Hidden Gems:

1. **Hundertwasser Village (Hundertwasser-Krawina-Haus)**: Located nearby, the Hundertwasser Village is another architectural gem designed by Hundertwasser and architect Peter Pelikan. This residential building features colorful facades, irregular forms, and a unique design that reflects Hundertwasser's artistic philosophy.

2. **Kunst Haus Wien Café**: After exploring the Hundertwasserhaus and museum, visitors can relax and enjoy a meal or refreshments at the Kunst Haus Wien Café, known for its cozy ambiance, artistic décor, and garden terrace.

3. **Hundertwasser Fountain**: Just a short walk from the Hundertwasserhaus, visitors can discover the Hundertwasser Fountain, a public artwork designed by Hundertwasser, featuring colorful mosaics, ceramic tiles, and a unique sculptural design that adds vibrancy to the surrounding area.

4. **Landstraßer Hauptstraße**: Explore the vibrant Landstraßer Hauptstraße, the main shopping street in the Landstraße

district, featuring a mix of boutiques, shops, cafes, and restaurants. Stroll along this bustling street, soak up the local atmosphere, and discover hidden gems, historic landmarks, and charming neighborhoods nearby.

5. **Stadtpark (City Park)**: Located within walking distance, the Stadtpark is one of Vienna's most beautiful parks, featuring lush green spaces, tranquil ponds, scenic pathways, and iconic landmarks like the Johann Strauss Monument and Kursalon Wien. Enjoy a leisurely stroll, relax by the water, or attend outdoor events and concerts in this picturesque urban oasis.

Kunsthistorisches Museum:

The Kunsthistorisches Museum (Museum of Art History) is located in Vienna, Austria, near the famous Ringstrasse and adjacent to the Natural History Museum (Naturhistorisches Museum). Here's a description of the location, tourist highlights, and hidden gems of the Kunsthistorisches Museum:

Location:

- **Address**: Maria-Theresien-Platz, 1010 Wien, Austria
- **Neighborhood**: The museum is situated in the historic center of Vienna, surrounded by prominent landmarks, cultural institutions, parks, and attractions, making it easily accessible by public transportation, walking, or cycling.

Tourist Highlights:

1. **Art Collections**: The Kunsthistorisches Museum houses an extensive collection of European art, including masterpieces by renowned artists such as Raphael, Vermeer, Caravaggio, Rembrandt, Velázquez, and Pieter Bruegel the Elder.

2. **Grand Staircase and Cupola Hall**: Admire the stunning architecture, grand staircase, and Cupola Hall adorned with frescoes, sculptures, and intricate details that showcase the museum's Baroque design and elegance.
3. **Egyptian and Near Eastern Collection**: Explore the museum's vast collection of ancient Egyptian, Near Eastern, and Classical artifacts, including statues, mummies, sarcophagi, jewelry, and archaeological treasures.
4. **Picture Gallery**: Discover the Picture Gallery featuring a diverse collection of paintings, portraits, landscapes, and religious artworks spanning the Renaissance, Baroque, and other periods of European art history.
5. **Special Exhibitions**: Attend temporary exhibitions, curated displays, educational programs, and events that highlight specific themes, artists, periods, or cultural topics related to the museum's collections.

Hidden Gems:

1. **Coin Cabinet (Münzkabinett)**: Visit the Coin Cabinet, located within the museum, showcasing an extensive collection of coins, medals, numismatic artifacts, and historical currency from ancient times to the modern era.
2. **Kunstkammer Wien**: Explore the Kunstkammer Wien, a unique museum within the museum, featuring a collection of artworks, curiosities, precious objects, sculptures, and historical artifacts from the Renaissance and Baroque periods.
3. **Architectural Details**: Take time to appreciate the museum's architectural details, decorative elements, and hidden gems, including ornate ceilings, stucco work, sculptures, and intricate designs that enhance the visitor's experience and appreciation of the Baroque artistry.
4. **Museum Café and Shop**: Relax and unwind at the museum café, enjoy a coffee, snack, or meal, and explore

the museum shop offering a wide range of art books, souvenirs, gifts, and exclusive merchandise related to the museum's collections and exhibitions.

Chapter 3:
Itineraries

Creating an itinerary for your visit to Vienna is essential for maximizing time, optimizing resources, experiencing diversity, immersing in culture, embracing flexibility, leveraging local insights, ensuring safety and comfort, and capturing memorable moments that resonate with authenticity, depth, meaning, and significance. By planning thoughtfully, exploring mindfully, engaging respectfully, and embracing Vienna's enchanting spirit, soul, energy, and essence, you embark on a transformative, enriching, and unforgettable journey that celebrates the city's enduring allure, hospitality, warmth, authenticity, and contributions to history, culture, art, music, cuisine, innovation, and global community.

One week itinerary

Day 1: Arrival and Orientation

- **Morning**: Arrive in Vienna, check into your accommodation, and take a leisurely stroll around your neighborhood to familiarize yourself with the surroundings.

- **Afternoon**: Visit the **Vienna State Opera** to admire its stunning architecture and attend a guided tour or performance if available.
- **Evening**: Enjoy dinner at a traditional Viennese restaurant, sampling local specialties like Wiener Schnitzel, Tafelspitz, or Apfelstrudel.

Day 2: Historic Landmarks and Palaces

- **Morning**: Explore **Schönbrunn Palace**, including the palace rooms, gardens, Gloriette, and the Tiergarten (Zoo).
- **Afternoon**: Visit the **Hofburg Palace** complex, including the Imperial Apartments, Sisi Museum, Imperial Silver Collection, and Spanish Riding School.
- **Evening**: Attend a classical concert, opera, or ballet performance at a historic venue like the Musikverein or Konzerthaus.

Day 3: Museums and Art Galleries

- **Morning**: Spend the morning exploring the **Kunsthistorisches Museum** and its diverse art collections, including paintings, sculptures, and decorative arts.
- **Afternoon**: Visit the **Belvedere Palace** complex, explore the Upper and Lower Belvedere, and admire iconic artworks like Gustav Klimt's "The Kiss."
- **Evening**: Enjoy dinner at Naschmarkt, Vienna's famous open-air market, and sample international cuisines, fresh produce, and gourmet foods.

Day 4: Cultural and Musical Heritage

- **Morning**: Explore the **Vienna Woods (Wienerwald)**, take a scenic hike, bike ride, or leisurely stroll through this picturesque forested area.

- **Afternoon**: Visit the **House of Music (Haus der Musik)**, explore interactive exhibits, musical instruments, sound installations, and Vienna's musical heritage.
- **Evening**: Attend a performance at the Vienna State Opera or explore the vibrant nightlife, bars, and cafes in the city center.

Day 5: Vienna's Parks and Green Spaces

- **Morning**: Visit the **Vienna Prater**, enjoy rides, attractions, and panoramic views from the Giant Ferris Wheel (Riesenrad).
- **Afternoon**: Explore **Stadtpark**, relax by the pond, admire the Johann Strauss Monument, and stroll through this beautiful park featuring gardens, pathways, and sculptures.
- **Evening**: Dine at a Heuriger (wine tavern) in Grinzing or Neustift am Walde, enjoy local wines, traditional Austrian dishes, and live music.

Day 6: Shopping and Leisure

- **Morning**: Shop and stroll along **Graben and Kohlmarkt**, Vienna's prestigious shopping streets, featuring luxury boutiques, international brands, and elegant storefronts.
- **Afternoon**: Explore the **MuseumsQuartier (MQ)**, visit art museums, galleries, exhibition spaces, and enjoy a leisurely afternoon exploring this vibrant cultural district.
- **Evening**: Attend a performance, concert, or event at the MQ, or dine at a trendy restaurant, cafe, or rooftop bar with panoramic city views.

Day 7: Departure and Farewell

- **Morning**: Visit any remaining attractions, landmarks, or neighborhoods on your bucket list, and enjoy a final stroll through the city center.

- **Afternoon**: Check out of your accommodation, shop for last-minute souvenirs, gifts, or treats at local markets or shops.
- **Evening**: Depart from Vienna, reflecting on your memorable week exploring the city's history, culture, art, cuisine, and vibrant atmosphere.

Two weeks itinerary

Week 1: Explore Vienna's Landmarks and Cultural Attractions

Day 1: Arrival and Orientation

- **Morning**: Arrive in Vienna, check into your accommodation, and take a leisurely walk around your neighborhood.
- **Afternoon**: Explore the **Vienna State Opera** and attend a guided tour or performance.
- **Evening**: Enjoy dinner at a traditional Viennese restaurant and relax after your journey.

Day 2: Historic Palaces and Museums

- **Morning**: Visit **Schönbrunn Palace**, including the palace rooms, gardens, and zoo.
- **Afternoon**: Explore the **Hofburg Palace** complex, including the Imperial Apartments, Sisi Museum, and Spanish Riding School.
- **Evening**: Attend a classical concert, opera, or ballet performance.

Day 3: Art and History Museums

- **Morning**: Explore the **Kunsthistorisches Museum** and its diverse art collections.

- **Afternoon**: Visit the **Belvedere Palace**, including the Upper and Lower Belvedere, and admire artworks like Gustav Klimt's "The Kiss."
- **Evening**: Dinner at Naschmarkt, Vienna's famous open-air market.

Day 4: Parks and Leisure Activities

- **Morning**: Explore **Vienna Prater** and enjoy rides, attractions, and panoramic views.
- **Afternoon**: Relax at **Stadtpark**, explore gardens, sculptures, and leisurely walkways.
- **Evening**: Dine at a Heuriger (wine tavern) in Grinzing or Neustift am Walde.

Day 5: Music and Cultural Heritage

- **Morning**: Visit the **House of Music (Haus der Musik)** and explore interactive exhibits and Vienna's musical heritage.
- **Afternoon**: Attend a guided tour of the **Vienna State Opera** or explore the backstage areas and historical archives.
- **Evening**: Attend a performance at the Vienna State Opera or explore the city's nightlife.

Day 6: Neighborhood Exploration

- **Morning**: Explore the historic district of **Innere Stadt**, including Graben, Kohlmarkt, and Stephansplatz.
- **Afternoon**: Visit the **MuseumsQuartier (MQ)**, explore art museums, galleries, and cultural institutions.
- **Evening**: Dine at a local restaurant, cafe, or rooftop bar with panoramic city views.

Day 7: Day Trip to Bratislava or Danube Valley

- **Full Day**: Take a day trip to Bratislava, Slovakia, or explore the scenic Danube Valley, including Krems, Dürnstein, and Melk.
- **Evening**: Return to Vienna, relax, and enjoy dinner at a restaurant specializing in Austrian cuisine.

Week 2: Day Trips, Culinary Experiences, and Relaxation

Day 8-10: Day Trips and Nearby Attractions

- **Day 8**: Explore the Wachau Valley, visit vineyards, sample local wines, and enjoy scenic views along the Danube River.
- **Day 9**: Take a day trip to Salzburg, birthplace of Mozart, explore the old town, Hohensalzburg Fortress, and Sound of Music locations.
- **Day 10**: Relax and unwind at a local spa, wellness center, or thermal baths near Vienna, such as Baden bei Wien or Lázně.

Day 11-14: Culinary Experiences and Leisure Activities

- **Day 11**: Participate in a cooking class, food tour, or culinary workshop to learn about Austrian cuisine, traditional dishes, and culinary traditions.
- **Day 12**: Explore Vienna's coffeehouse culture, visit historic cafes, and enjoy traditional Viennese coffee, cakes, and pastries.
- **Day 13**: Visit the Vienna Woods (Wienerwald), enjoy hiking, cycling, or outdoor activities in this picturesque forested area.
- **Day 14**: Shop for souvenirs, gifts, and treats at local markets, artisan shops, and boutiques, and enjoy a farewell dinner at a top-rated restaurant.

Departure: Farewell Vienna

- **Morning**: Visit any remaining attractions, landmarks, or neighborhoods on your bucket list, and enjoy a final stroll through the city center.
- **Afternoon**: Check out of your accommodation, shop for last-minute souvenirs, and depart from Vienna, reflecting on your memorable two-week journey.

Weekend itinerary

Day 1: Arrival and Historic Landmarks

Morning:

- **Arrival**: Arrive in Vienna and check into your accommodation.
- **Orientation**: Take a leisurely walk around the city center, explore Stephansplatz, and admire St. Stephen's Cathedral (Stephansdom).

Afternoon:

- **Historic Landmarks**: Visit the Hofburg Palace complex, including the Imperial Apartments, Sisi Museum, and Spanish Riding School.
- **Café Culture**: Experience Vienna's coffeehouse culture, enjoy a traditional Viennese coffee, and indulge in Sachertorte or Apfelstrudel at a historic café like Café Central or Café Sacher.

Evening:

- **Dinner**: Dine at a traditional Viennese restaurant, sample local specialties like Wiener Schnitzel, Tafelspitz, or Kaiserschmarrn.
- **Nightlife**: Explore Vienna's vibrant nightlife, visit a wine tavern (Heuriger) in Grinzing or Neustift am Walde, or

enjoy a performance at the Vienna State Opera or Musikverein.

Day 2: Museums, Art, and Culture

Morning:

- **Art Museums**: Visit the Kunsthistorisches Museum or Belvedere Palace, explore art collections, masterpieces, and exhibitions featuring renowned artists like Gustav Klimt, Egon Schiele, and more.
- **MuseumQuartier**: Explore the MuseumsQuartier (MQ), visit art museums, galleries, and cultural institutions, and enjoy the vibrant atmosphere of this cultural district.

Afternoon:

- **Historic Palaces**: Explore Schönbrunn Palace, including the palace rooms, gardens, and Gloriette, or visit another historic palace like Belvedere or Hofburg for a guided tour or self-exploration.
- **Shopping**: Stroll along Graben and Kohlmarkt, Vienna's prestigious shopping streets, featuring luxury boutiques, international brands, and elegant storefronts.

Evening:

- **Dinner**: Dine at a trendy restaurant, rooftop bar, or traditional Austrian eatery, and enjoy culinary delights, local wines, and Austrian hospitality.
- **Entertainment**: Attend a classical concert, opera, or ballet performance at a historic venue like the Vienna State Opera, Musikverein, or Volksoper.

Day 3: Parks, Leisure, and Departure

Morning:

- **Parks and Gardens**: Explore the Vienna Prater, enjoy rides, attractions, and panoramic views from the Giant Ferris Wheel (Riesenrad), or relax at Stadtpark and explore gardens, sculptures, and leisurely walkways.
- **Outdoor Activities**: Rent a bike, take a guided tour, or explore the Danube River, Vienna Woods, or nearby parks and green spaces for outdoor activities and recreational fun.

Afternoon:

- **Shopping and Souvenirs**: Visit Naschmarkt, shop for souvenirs, gifts, and treats at local markets, artisan shops, and boutiques.
- **Farewell Lunch**: Enjoy a farewell lunch at a top-rated restaurant, café, or traditional eatery, savoring Austrian cuisine, local specialties, and regional flavors.

Departure:

- **Departure**: Check out of your accommodation, shop for last-minute souvenirs or treats, and depart from Vienna, reflecting on your memorable weekend exploring the city's history, culture, art, and vibrant atmosphere.

Chapter 4:
Best Restaurants and Cuisine

Viennese cuisine is a delightful blend of traditional Austrian dishes, regional specialties, and international influences, reflecting the city's rich history, cultural heritage, and culinary traditions. Vienna offers a diverse range of flavors, ingredients, and culinary delights that tantalize your taste buds and satisfy your appetite. Here's a description of Vienna's cuisine and 15 must-try local dishes for visitors:

Vienna Cuisine:

- **Traditional Austrian Dishes**: Vienna's cuisine features hearty and flavorful dishes, including meats (pork, beef, veal), dumplings, potatoes, sauces, and gravies, often accompanied by fresh vegetables, herbs, and spices.
- **Coffeehouse Culture**: Vienna is renowned for its coffeehouse culture, offering a variety of coffee drinks, pastries, cakes, and desserts that are perfect for breakfast, afternoon tea, or a sweet treat.

- **Wine and Schnapps**: Vienna's culinary scene includes a wide selection of Austrian wines, beers, schnapps, and alcoholic beverages produced locally or sourced from renowned vineyards and breweries across Austria.
- **Seasonal and Local Ingredients**: Vienna's cuisine emphasizes fresh, seasonal, and locally sourced ingredients, including fruits, vegetables, meats, cheeses, bread, and dairy products, reflecting the city's commitment to quality, sustainability, and traditional farming practices.

15 Must-Try Local Cuisine in Vienna:

1. **Wiener Schnitzel**: A classic Viennese dish featuring breaded and fried veal or pork cutlets, served with lemon, parsley, potato salad, or potato fries.
2. **Apfelstrudel**: A popular Austrian dessert made with thin layers of flaky pastry filled with spiced apples, raisins, cinnamon, sugar, and breadcrumbs, served warm with powdered sugar and vanilla sauce.
3. **Sachertorte**: Vienna's famous chocolate cake featuring layers of dense chocolate cake, apricot jam, and dark chocolate icing, served with whipped cream.
4. **Tafelspitz**: A traditional Austrian dish consisting of boiled beef or veal, served with horseradish sauce, apple-horseradish sauce, boiled potatoes, and vegetables.
5. **Kaiserschmarrn**: A fluffy shredded pancake dessert served with powdered sugar, fruit compote (usually plum or apple), and sometimes rum-soaked raisins.
6. **Goulash**: A hearty and flavorful stew made with beef, onions, paprika, tomatoes, potatoes, and spices, often served with bread, dumplings, or noodles.
7. **Erdäpfelsalat**: Viennese potato salad made with boiled potatoes, onions, vinegar, mustard, oil, seasonings, and fresh herbs, served as a side dish or accompaniment to meats and sausages.

8. **Beuschel**: A traditional Viennese ragout made with veal lungs and heart, cooked with onions, garlic, vinegar, cream, and spices, often served with bread dumplings or potatoes.

9. **Brettljause**: A rustic Austrian snack platter featuring a selection of cold cuts (ham, bacon, sausage), cheeses, pickles, bread, butter, horseradish, and mustard, perfect for sharing or as an appetizer.

10. **Topfenknödel**: Sweet dumplings made with quark (soft cheese), eggs, flour, breadcrumbs, sugar, and vanilla, served warm with fruit sauce, melted butter, and powdered sugar.

11. **Schnitzel Wiener Art**: A variation of Wiener Schnitzel made with pork or veal, breaded, fried, and served with potato salad, cranberry sauce, and lemon wedges.

12. **Käsekrainer**: A popular Austrian sausage filled with cheese (Emmental or Swiss cheese), grilled or fried, and served with mustard, horseradish, bread, or sauerkraut.

13. **Palatschinken**: Viennese-style crepes filled with sweet or savory fillings, such as apricot jam, Nutella, fresh fruits, whipped cream, cheese, ham, or mushrooms, and served as a dessert or main dish.

14. **Mohnnudeln**: Sweet poppy seed noodles made with ground poppy seeds, flour, butter, sugar, and milk, shaped into dumplings, boiled, and served with melted butter and powdered sugar.

15. **Austrian Wines and Beers**: Sample a variety of Austrian wines (Grüner Veltliner, Zweigelt, Blaufränkisch) and beers (Stiegl, Gösser, Ottakringer) produced locally or sourced from renowned vineyards and breweries across Austria.

Restaurants

Vienna offers a diverse range of eateries, from traditional Austrian taverns and coffeehouses to fine dining restaurants and international cuisine. Here are five renowned eatery options in each category, highlighting their services and specialties:

Traditional Austrian Taverns (Beisl):

1. **Figlmüller**: Known for its iconic Wiener Schnitzel, Figlmüller offers a cozy and traditional Viennese atmosphere with classic Austrian dishes, wines, and desserts.
   - **Services**: Reservations recommended, casual dining, seasonal menu, vegetarian options.
2. **Plachutta**: Specializing in Tafelspitz (boiled beef), Plachutta offers a rustic and authentic Austrian dining experience with hearty dishes, soups, and desserts.
   - **Services**: Reservations essential, family-friendly, private dining, traditional décor.
3. **Zum Schwarzen Kameel**: Established in 1618, Zum Schwarzen Kameel offers a historic setting, traditional Austrian cuisine, open-faced sandwiches, pastries, and a famous wine bar.
   - **Services**: Elegant dining, café, wine bar, catering, private events.
4. **Reinthaler's Beisl**: Located near St. Stephen's Cathedral, Reinthaler's Beisl offers traditional Austrian dishes, daily specials, homemade desserts, and a cozy, welcoming atmosphere.
   - **Services**: Casual dining, lunch specials, outdoor seating, vegetarian-friendly.
5. **Wrenkh**: Known for its innovative and vegetarian-friendly Austrian cuisine, Wrenkh offers a modern twist on classic dishes, fresh ingredients, and creative presentations.
   - **Services**: Fine dining, vegetarian options, cooking classes, wine pairing, seasonal menu.

Coffeehouses and Cafés:

1. **Café Central**: A historic coffeehouse since 1876, Café Central offers classic Viennese coffee, pastries, cakes, and a grand ambiance with vaulted ceilings and elegant décor.
   - **Services**: Breakfast, brunch, dessert, outdoor seating, live piano music.
2. **Demel**: Founded in 1786, Demel is famous for its artisanal pastries, chocolates, cakes, and traditional Viennese coffeehouse specialties.
   - **Services**: Bakery, café, afternoon tea, gift shop, private events.
3. **Café Sacher**: Home of the world-famous Sachertorte, Café Sacher offers a luxurious and elegant setting, traditional coffeehouse culture, and a wide selection of desserts, pastries, and beverages.
   - **Services**: Dessert shop, breakfast, lunch, dinner, outdoor seating, gift shop.
4. **Aida Café**: A classic Viennese café chain, Aida offers colorful interiors, traditional coffee drinks, pastries, sandwiches, and a nostalgic atmosphere reminiscent of the 1950s.
   - **Services**: Casual dining, bakery, coffeehouse, takeaway, seasonal specials.
5. **Kaffee Alt Wien**: Located in the historic city center, Kaffee Alt Wien offers a traditional Viennese coffeehouse experience with classic coffee drinks, homemade pastries, snacks, and a cozy, relaxed ambiance.
   - **Services**: Coffeehouse, breakfast, lunch, dessert, free Wi-Fi, outdoor seating.

Fine Dining and International Cuisine:

1. **Steirereck**: A two-Michelin-starred restaurant, Steirereck offers innovative Austrian cuisine, seasonal ingredients, tasting menus, wine pairings, and a luxurious dining

experience.

- **Services**: Fine dining, tasting menu, wine pairing, vegetarian options, private dining.

2. **Konstantin Filippou**: Combining Austrian and Mediterranean flavors, Konstantin Filippou offers creative dishes, seasonal ingredients, tasting menus, and a contemporary dining atmosphere.
   - **Services**: Fine dining, Michelin-starred, tasting menu, wine pairing, private events.

3. **Edvard**: Located in the Kempinski Hotel, Edvard offers gourmet European cuisine, seasonal menus, wine pairings, and a sophisticated dining experience with elegant décor and ambiance.
   - **Services**: Fine dining, Michelin-starred, tasting menu, wine pairing, private dining.

4. **TIAN**: A renowned vegetarian restaurant, TIAN offers innovative and sustainable plant-based cuisine, tasting menus, organic ingredients, and a modern, stylish dining setting.
   - **Services**: Fine dining, vegetarian, tasting menu, wine pairing, sustainable.

5. **Mraz & Sohn**: Known for its modern Austrian cuisine, Mraz & Sohn offers creative dishes, tasting menus, seasonal ingredients, and a relaxed yet elegant dining experience with a focus on innovation and flavor.
   - **Services**: Fine dining, tasting menu, wine pairing, vegetarian options, contemporary décor.

Chapter 5:
Accommodations in Vienna

Vienna offers a diverse range of accommodation options to suit every traveler's preference, budget, and needs, from luxurious five-star hotels to boutique guesthouses, budget-friendly hostels, and apartment rentals. Here are five renowned examples in each category with a brief description of their services:

Luxury Hotels:

1. **Hotel Sacher Wien**:
   - **Services**: Elegant rooms and suites, gourmet restaurants, spa and wellness facilities, concierge services, afternoon tea, and personalized guest services in a historic and luxurious setting.
2. **Park Hyatt Vienna**:
   - **Services**: Stylish accommodations, fine dining restaurants, luxury spa, fitness center, business

amenities, personal butler service, and exclusive experiences in a prime location near popular attractions.

3. **The Ritz-Carlton, Vienna:**
   - **Services**: Sophisticated rooms and suites, rooftop bar, gourmet dining options, wellness center, event spaces, personalized services, and luxurious amenities for a memorable stay in Vienna.

4. **Hotel Imperial, a Luxury Collection Hotel, Vienna:**
   - **Services**: Opulent accommodations, Michelin-starred restaurant, cocktail bar, spa treatments, event venues, personalized services, and historical charm in a prestigious setting.

5. **Palais Coburg Residenz:**
   - **Services**: Grand suites, gourmet dining experiences, wine cellar tours, private garden, spa and wellness facilities, concierge services, and exclusive amenities in a historic palace setting.

Mid-Range Hotels:

1. **Hotel Sans Souci Wien:**
   - **Services**: Boutique accommodations, gourmet restaurant, wellness center, art gallery, personalized services, and contemporary design in a central location.

2. **25hours Hotel beim MuseumsQuartier:**
   - **Services**: Unique themed rooms, rooftop bar, restaurant, fitness center, bicycle rentals, event spaces, and vibrant atmosphere near MuseumsQuartier.

3. **Hotel de France Wien:**
   - **Services**: Comfortable rooms, multiple dining options, wellness center, business amenities, event venues, and convenient location near Ringstrasse.

4. **Hotel König von Ungarn:**
   - **Services**: Historic accommodations, traditional

Viennese charm, gourmet breakfast, concierge services, and personalized guest experiences near Stephansplatz.

5. **Hotel Am Konzerthaus Vienna - MGallery**:
   - **Services**: Contemporary rooms, gourmet restaurant, wellness center, event spaces, personalized services, and prime location near Belvedere Palace.

Budget-Friendly Options:

1. **Wombat's City Hostel Vienna - The Naschmarkt**:
   - **Services**: Affordable dormitory and private rooms, communal kitchen, rooftop terrace, social events, bicycle rentals, and lively atmosphere near Naschmarkt.
2. **A&O Wien Stadthalle**:
   - **Services**: Budget-friendly accommodations, dormitory and private rooms, bar, lounge, game room, bicycle rentals, and convenient location near Westbahnhof.
3. **Meininger Hotel Wien Downtown Franz**:
   - **Services**: Modern accommodations, dormitory and private rooms, guest kitchen, game zone, bicycle rentals, and social areas near the city center.
4. **Hostel Ruthensteiner Vienna**:
   - **Services**: Cozy accommodations, dormitory and private rooms, communal kitchen, garden terrace, social events, and welcoming atmosphere near Westbahnhof.
5. **Wombats City Hostel Vienna - The Lounge**:
   - **Services**: Budget-friendly dormitory and private rooms, rooftop terrace, communal areas, social events, and vibrant atmosphere near Mariahilfer Strasse.

Chapter 6:
Cultural Activities in Vienna

Vienna, known as the "City of Music" and "City of Dreams," offers a rich cultural tapestry that invites visitors to immerse themselves in its artistic, historical, and intellectual heritage. Here are 15 cultural activities visitors can enjoy in Vienna:

1. **Vienna State Opera**: Experience world-class opera, ballet, and classical concerts at the Vienna State Opera, one of the leading opera houses globally, renowned for its stunning architecture and performances.
2. **Vienna Philharmonic Orchestra**: Attend a concert by the Vienna Philharmonic Orchestra, one of the world's most prestigious orchestras, performing symphonies, chamber music, and classical masterpieces.
3. **Musikverein**: Visit the Musikverein, Vienna's iconic concert hall, home to the Vienna Philharmonic's New Year's Concert, and enjoy classical music performances,

chamber music, and recitals.

4. **MuseumsQuartier (MQ)**: Explore the MuseumsQuartier, Vienna's vibrant cultural district, featuring art museums, galleries, exhibition spaces, cultural institutions, festivals, and events throughout the year.

5. **Belvedere Palace**: Discover the Belvedere Palace complex, including the Upper and Lower Belvedere, and admire iconic artworks like Gustav Klimt's "The Kiss" and other Austrian masterpieces.

6. **Schönbrunn Palace**: Explore Schönbrunn Palace, a UNESCO World Heritage Site, featuring royal apartments, gardens, the Gloriette, and the world's oldest zoo, offering a glimpse into Vienna's imperial history.

7. **Hofburg Palace**: Visit the Hofburg Palace, the former imperial palace of the Habsburg dynasty, and explore museums, the Spanish Riding School, Imperial Apartments, and historical collections.

8. **Vienna Boys' Choir**: Attend a performance by the Vienna Boys' Choir, one of the oldest and most renowned boys' choirs in the world, known for its angelic voices and musical excellence.

9. **Albertina Museum**: Explore the Albertina Museum, one of Vienna's most prestigious art museums, featuring a vast collection of prints, drawings, photographs, and temporary exhibitions by renowned artists.

10. **Vienna State Opera Ball**: Experience the glamour and elegance of the Vienna State Opera Ball, one of the most prestigious and celebrated social events, featuring waltzes, ballroom dancing, and cultural traditions.

11. **Vienna Coffeehouse Culture**: Indulge in Vienna's coffeehouse culture, visit historic cafes like Café Central, Café Sacher, and Café Hawelka, and enjoy traditional Viennese coffee, pastries, and desserts.

12. **Naschmarkt**: Wander through Naschmarkt, Vienna's most popular market, featuring diverse stalls, international cuisines, gourmet foods, spices, fresh produce, antiques,

and flea market treasures.

13. **Jewish Vienna**: Explore Jewish Vienna, visit the Jewish Museum, Holocaust Memorial, Jewish Quarter, and synagogues, and learn about Vienna's Jewish history, heritage, culture, and contributions.

14. **Vienna Woods (Wienerwald)**: Escape the city and explore the Vienna Woods, a picturesque forested area offering hiking trails, scenic views, outdoor activities, and natural beauty.

15. **Danube River Cruise**: Enjoy a scenic Danube River cruise, exploring Vienna's waterfront, historic landmarks, picturesque landscapes, and experiencing the city from a unique perspective.

Chapter 7:
Nightlife And Festivals In Vienna

Vienna boasts a vibrant and diverse nightlife scene that caters to a range of tastes, preferences, and interests, from sophisticated cocktail bars and trendy nightclubs to cozy wine taverns and cultural venues. Here are ten nightlife destinations in Vienna and what visitors can enjoy:

1. Bermuda Bräu:

- **Location**: Situated in Vienna's city center, Bermuda Bräu is a popular brewpub known for its authentic Austrian beer culture.
- **What to Enjoy**: Visitors can savor a variety of craft beers brewed on-site, indulge in hearty pub food like schnitzel and sausages, and enjoy live music performances ranging from traditional folk to contemporary rock.

2. Das Loft:

- **Location**: Perched atop the Sofitel Vienna Stephansdom, Das Loft offers breathtaking panoramic views of the city skyline.
- **What to Enjoy**: Guests can unwind with innovative cocktails crafted by expert mixologists, dine on gourmet cuisine featuring local and international flavors, groove to DJ sets featuring eclectic music genres, and experience a chic ambiance that blends sophistication with modern design.

3. Flex:

- **Location**: Located along the Danube Canal, Flex is a legendary nightclub and concert venue renowned for its diverse music scene.
- **What to Enjoy**: Nightlife enthusiasts can dance to the beats of international DJs, attend live concerts featuring local and international artists, participate in themed parties, and enjoy the club's vibrant atmosphere that caters to a diverse crowd of music lovers and partygoers.

4. Rote Bar:

- **Location**: Nestled within the historic Volkstheater, Rote Bar exudes elegance and charm, offering a sophisticated nightlife experience.
- **What to Enjoy**: Guests can sip on classic cocktails, fine wines, and champagne while enjoying live jazz, piano performances, or cabaret shows in an intimate setting that transports you back to Vienna's golden era of elegance and refinement.

5. Motto am Fluss:

- **Location**: Situated by the Danube Canal, Motto am Fluss offers a trendy riverside setting perfect for socializing and enjoying the scenic views.

- **What to Enjoy**: Visitors can dine on gourmet cuisine featuring fresh seafood, local ingredients, and international flavors, sip on creative cocktails crafted by skilled bartenders, relax on the outdoor terrace, and soak in the vibrant atmosphere of Vienna's bustling waterfront.

6. Ottakringer Brauerei:

- **Location**: Located in the Ottakring district, Ottakringer Brauerei is Vienna's largest brewery and a hub for beer enthusiasts.
- **What to Enjoy**: Beer aficionados can join guided brewery tours, participate in beer tastings, attend seasonal festivals and events, dine on traditional Austrian dishes, and relax in the beer garden while enjoying live music and entertainment.

7. Prater Sauna:

- **Location**: Situated in Vienna's LGBTQ+ nightlife scene, Prater Sauna offers a welcoming and inclusive atmosphere for all guests.
- **What to Enjoy**: Visitors can unwind in steam rooms, saunas, and relaxation areas, participate in themed parties and events, enjoy cocktails and refreshments at the bar, and socialize in a friendly and diverse environment that celebrates individuality, acceptance, and community.

8. Tür 7:

- **Location**: Tucked away behind a secret door inside the 7*stern café, Tür 7 offers a unique and intimate speakeasy experience.
- **What to Enjoy**: Guests can discover this hidden gem, enjoy inventive cocktails crafted with precision and creativity,

soak in the intimate ambiance, and savor a nightlife experience that combines mystery, sophistication, and exclusivity.

9. Volksgarten:

- **Location**: Located in the heart of Vienna, Volksgarten is a historic park and nightclub offering a blend of outdoor and indoor nightlife experiences.
- **What to Enjoy**: Nightlife enthusiasts can dance under the stars in the outdoor garden, attend themed parties featuring international DJs, relax in lounge areas, and enjoy the club's vibrant atmosphere that caters to a diverse crowd of music lovers and partygoers.

10. WerkzeugH:

- **Location**: Situated in a former factory, WerkzeugH is a cultural venue and nightclub offering an alternative nightlife experience in Vienna.
- **What to Enjoy**: Visitors can explore art exhibitions, attend live concerts featuring local and international artists, dance to DJ sets featuring electronic music, participate in themed events, and enjoy the venue's unique industrial-chic ambiance that blends creativity, culture, and nightlife.

Festivals

Vienna hosts a variety of festivals throughout the year, celebrating music, arts, culture, culinary delights, traditions, and more. Here are 20 festivals visitors can enjoy in Vienna, along with what to enjoy, when, and where they happen:

1. Vienna Opera Ball (February):

The Vienna Opera Ball is the epitome of elegance and grandeur, transforming the Vienna State Opera into a glamorous ballroom filled with waltzes, ballroom dancing, live orchestras, and a sea of elegantly dressed attendees. Visitors can purchase tickets for the ball or enjoy the atmosphere outside the opera house, watching the arrival of guests, and soaking up the festive ambiance of this iconic event.

2. Vienna Festival (May-June):

The Vienna Festival showcases a diverse range of international artists, theater productions, music genres, dance styles, and cultural expressions across various venues in the city. Visitors can explore the festival program, attend performances, exhibitions, workshops, and events, and immerse themselves in Vienna's vibrant arts scene during this annual celebration of creativity, innovation, and artistic excellence.

3. Life Ball (June):

The Life Ball is Europe's largest charity event supporting HIV/AIDS research, awareness, and prevention, featuring celebrity guests, fashion shows, musical performances, art installations, and a vibrant parade through Vienna's streets. Visitors can purchase tickets, participate in fundraising activities, attend themed parties, and contribute to a worthy cause while enjoying the festivities, costumes, and energy of this iconic event.

4. Vienna Jazz Festival (June-July):

The Vienna Jazz Festival showcases renowned jazz musicians, emerging artists, bands, and ensembles performing at historic venues, concert halls, jazz clubs, and outdoor stages across the city. Visitors can explore the festival lineup, attend concerts, jam sessions, workshops, and events, and experience Vienna's rich jazz heritage, improvisational spirit, and musical creativity during this annual celebration of jazz culture.

5. Vienna Pride (June):

Vienna Pride is a vibrant LGBTQ+ festival celebrating diversity, equality, inclusion, and human rights through parades, parties, concerts, art exhibitions, film screenings, workshops, and events throughout the city. Visitors can participate in the Pride Parade, explore Pride Village at Rathausplatz, attend cultural events, support LGBTQ+ organizations, and enjoy the inclusive and festive atmosphere of Vienna Pride.

6. ImPulsTanz - Vienna International Dance Festival (July-August):

ImPulsTanz is one of Europe's leading dance festivals, featuring contemporary dance performances, choreographic explorations, workshops, masterclasses, and events showcasing innovative dance artists, companies, and productions. Visitors can attend dance shows, participate in workshops, meet artists, explore different dance styles and techniques, and immerse themselves in Vienna's dynamic and diverse dance community during this annual festival.

7. Vienna Film Festival – Viennale (October):

The Viennale is Vienna's premier film festival, showcasing international films, documentaries, retrospectives, premieres, and cinematic experiences at cinemas, theaters, cultural venues, and outdoor screenings across the city. Visitors can explore the festival program, attend film screenings, Q&A sessions, meet filmmakers, discover new cinematic voices, and experience Vienna's vibrant film culture during this annual celebration of storytelling, creativity, and cinematic artistry.

8. Vienna Wine Festival (Wiener Weinwandertage) (May & September):

The Wiener Weinwandertage invites visitors to explore Vienna's wine culture through vineyard tours, wine tastings, culinary pairings, outdoor activities, and events showcasing Austria's wine regions, varietals, and winemaking traditions. Visitors can hike through vineyards, meet winemakers, taste regional wines, enjoy panoramic views of Vienna, and experience the terroir, flavors, and hospitality of Austrian wine country during this annual wine festival.

9. Vienna Christmas Markets (Wiener Christkindlmarkt) (November-December):

Vienna's enchanting Christmas markets transform the city into a winter wonderland, featuring festive decorations, handcrafted gifts, artisanal products, traditional treats, mulled wine (Glühwein), holiday concerts, and seasonal festivities throughout November and December. Visitors can explore different markets, purchase unique gifts, enjoy festive foods, attend holiday concerts, and experience the magical atmosphere of Vienna's Christmas markets during the holiday season.

10. Vienna Mozart Week (January):

The Vienna Mozart Week celebrates Mozart's music and legacy through concerts, opera performances, chamber music, recitals, exhibitions, and events honoring the iconic composer's contributions to classical music. Visitors can attend Mozart-themed concerts, explore historical venues associated with Mozart, discover his life and works, and experience Vienna's enduring connection to Mozart's music and cultural heritage during this annual festival.

11. Vienna Coffee Festival (January):

The Vienna Coffee Festival celebrates Austria's rich coffee culture, heritage, and traditions through tastings, workshops, barista competitions, lectures, art exhibitions, and events showcasing Vienna's coffeehouses, roasters, and specialty coffee scene. Visitors can immerse themselves in Vienna's café culture, learn about coffee production, brewing methods, and enjoy aromatic blends, artisanal pastries, and coffee-inspired creations during this annual celebration of coffee craftsmanship and community.

12. Vienna Design Week (September-October):

Vienna Design Week showcases contemporary design, innovation, craftsmanship, and creativity through exhibitions, installations, workshops, talks, tours, and events across the city. Visitors can explore different design disciplines, meet designers, artists, and makers, discover innovative projects, and experience Vienna's vibrant design scene during this annual festival promoting sustainability, collaboration, and cultural exchange.

13. Vienna Festival of Old Music:

The Vienna Festival of Old Music celebrates Baroque, Renaissance, and Medieval music through concerts, recitals, chamber music, period instrument ensembles, workshops, and events showcasing historical repertoire, performance practices, and musical traditions. Visitors can attend performances in historic venues, explore early music interpretations, and experience Vienna's rich heritage of classical music during this annual festival honoring the music of past eras.

14. Vienna International Choir Festival & Competition:

The Vienna International Choir Festival & Competition brings together choirs from around the world to celebrate choral music, vocal arts, and cultural exchange through concerts, competitions, workshops, rehearsals, and events promoting musical excellence, collaboration, and community. Visitors can attend choir performances, participate in sing-alongs, meet choristers, and experience Vienna's vibrant choral scene during this annual festival uniting voices, cultures, and traditions.

15. Vienna Beer Week:

Vienna Beer Week celebrates Austria's brewing traditions, craft beer culture, and beer heritage through tastings, brewery tours, tap takeovers, beer pairing dinners, workshops, events, and festivities showcasing local breweries, artisanal beers, and beer-related activities across the city. Visitors can explore Vienna's craft beer scene, meet brewers, learn about beer production, and enjoy unique flavors, styles, and experiences during this annual celebration of brewing craftsmanship and community.

16. Vienna International Dance Week:

The Vienna International Dance Week features contemporary dance performances, choreographic explorations, workshops, masterclasses, lectures, and events showcasing innovative dance artists, companies, and productions from around the world. Visitors can attend dance shows, participate in workshops, meet choreographers, and experience Vienna's dynamic and diverse dance community during this annual festival promoting artistic excellence, creativity, and cultural exchange.

17. Vienna International Film Festival - Viennale:

The Viennale is Vienna's premier film festival, showcasing international films, documentaries, retrospectives, premieres, and cinematic experiences at cinemas, theaters, cultural venues, and outdoor screenings across the city. Visitors can explore the festival program, attend film screenings, Q&A sessions, meet filmmakers, discover new cinematic voices, and experience Vienna's vibrant film culture during this annual celebration of storytelling, creativity, and cinematic artistry.

18. Vienna Fashion Week:

Vienna Fashion Week highlights Austrian and international fashion designers, brands, trends, and styles through runway shows, presentations, exhibitions, pop-up shops, workshops, and events showcasing innovative collections, sustainable fashion, and emerging talents. Visitors can attend fashion shows, explore designer collections, meet industry professionals, and experience Vienna's evolving fashion scene during this annual event promoting creativity, innovation, and cultural expression.

19. Vienna Oktoberfest:

Vienna's Oktoberfest celebrates Bavarian culture, traditions, music, and cuisine through beer gardens, live music, folk dances, Bavarian specialties, games, contests, and festivities at various locations across the city. Visitors can enjoy Oktoberfest activities, sample German beers, savor authentic dishes, listen to traditional music, and experience Vienna's festive atmosphere during this annual celebration of Bavarian heritage, community, and camaraderie.

20. Vienna Literary Festival (Wiener Literaturfest):

The Vienna Literary Festival showcases Austrian and international authors, poets, storytellers, literary works, genres, and themes through readings, discussions, book signings, workshops, lectures, and events promoting literary excellence, creativity, and cultural exchange. Visitors can attend author talks, participate in literary events, explore book fairs, meet writers, and experience Vienna's vibrant literary scene during this annual festival celebrating the power of words, storytelling, and imagination.

Chapter 8:
Souvenirs And Shopping in Vienna

Shopping in Vienna is a delightful experience, offering visitors a blend of traditional markets, luxury boutiques, international brands, and unique shops that reflect the city's rich history, culture, and fashion-forward spirit. Here are ten shopping centers and districts in Vienna where visitors can enjoy diverse retail experiences:

1. **Kärntner Straße**: Located in the heart of Vienna's city center, Kärntner Straße is one of the most famous shopping streets featuring a mix of international retailers, department stores, luxury boutiques, souvenir shops, cafes, and restaurants. Visitors can explore Kärntner Straße's pedestrian-friendly promenade, shop for fashion, accessories, cosmetics, gifts, and enjoy the vibrant atmosphere of Vienna's bustling shopping district.

2. **Mariahilfer Straße**: Mariahilfer Straße is Vienna's longest and most popular shopping street, offering a diverse range of shops, boutiques, department stores, fashion brands,

designer labels, electronics, books, cafes, and eateries. Visitors can stroll along Mariahilfer Straße, shop for the latest trends, enjoy street performances, explore shopping malls, and experience Vienna's dynamic retail scene.

3. **The Ringstrassen-Galerien**: Located near the Vienna State Opera and Kärntner Straße, The Ringstrassen-Galerien is a luxury shopping arcade featuring high-end fashion boutiques, designer brands, jewelry stores, gourmet shops, cafes, restaurants, and a rooftop terrace with panoramic views of Vienna's city center. Visitors can shop for luxury goods, enjoy fine dining, and experience the elegance and sophistication of Vienna's premier shopping destination.

4. **Steffl Department Store**: Steffl Department Store is a historic shopping destination located on Kärntner Straße, offering a curated selection of international fashion brands, designer collections, luxury accessories, cosmetics, beauty products, gourmet foods, and home goods. Visitors can explore Steffl's multi-level store, shop for exclusive brands, enjoy personalized services, and discover Vienna's luxury retail experience.

5. **Naschmarkt**: Naschmarkt is Vienna's most popular open-air market, offering a vibrant mix of stalls, vendors, food stands, cafes, restaurants, antiques, crafts, spices, gourmet foods, fresh produce, flowers, and international cuisines. Visitors can explore Naschmarkt's bustling atmosphere, sample Austrian specialties, discover global flavors, and enjoy a culinary journey through Vienna's diverse food scene.

6. **The Mall Wien Mitte**: The Mall Wien Mitte is a modern shopping center located near Wien Mitte railway station, featuring a mix of fashion retailers, lifestyle brands, electronics, accessories, beauty products, services, cafes, restaurants, and a food court. Visitors can shop for the latest trends, enjoy dining options, access transportation links, and experience convenient shopping in Vienna's city center.

7. **Donau Zentrum**: Donau Zentrum is one of Vienna's largest shopping malls, offering a wide range of shops, boutiques, department stores, fashion brands, electronics, home goods, services, cinemas, restaurants, and entertainment options. Visitors can explore Donau Zentrum's diverse retail offerings, shop for fashion, accessories, gifts, enjoy leisure activities, and experience family-friendly shopping in Vienna's bustling district.

8. **Lugner City**: Lugner City is a shopping and entertainment complex located near the Westbahnhof railway station, featuring a mix of retailers, fashion brands, electronics, beauty salons, restaurants, cafes, cinemas, and entertainment venues. Visitors can shop for the latest trends, enjoy dining options, watch movies, and experience Vienna's dynamic shopping and entertainment scene.

9. **Millennium City**: Millennium City is a multifunctional complex located along the Danube River, featuring a shopping mall, entertainment center, cinema, fitness center, restaurants, cafes, and leisure facilities. Visitors can explore Millennium City's diverse retail offerings, shop for fashion, accessories, electronics, enjoy dining options, and experience entertainment activities in Vienna's modern district.

10. **Praterstraße and Leopoldstadt**: Praterstraße and Leopoldstadt are vibrant neighborhoods in Vienna, offering a mix of boutique shops, independent retailers, vintage stores, artisanal products, crafts, antiques, cafes, restaurants, and cultural attractions. Visitors can explore Praterstraße and Leopoldstadt's eclectic shopping scene, discover unique finds, support local businesses, enjoy culinary delights, and experience Vienna's diverse neighborhoods.

Souvenirs

Shopping for souvenirs in Vienna is a delightful experience, as the city offers a wide range of unique and authentic items that reflect its rich history, culture, craftsmanship, and traditions. Here are 15 must-buy souvenirs in Vienna that visitors can cherish as lasting memories of their trip:

1. **Mozartkugeln**: These are famous chocolate pralines named after Wolfgang Amadeus Mozart, the iconic composer who was born in Salzburg, Austria. Mozartkugeln are delicious marzipan-filled chocolates coated with nougat and dark chocolate, packaged in decorative wrappers, making them a popular souvenir from Vienna.

2. **Viennese Coffee**: Vienna is renowned for its coffeehouse culture, and visitors can purchase locally roasted coffee beans, ground coffee blends, and coffee-related products like espresso cups, mugs, and coffee accessories to enjoy Vienna's aromatic coffee at home.

3. **Wiener Porzellan (Viennese Porcelain)**: Vienna's porcelain is renowned for its quality, craftsmanship, and elegant designs. Visitors can purchase handcrafted porcelain figurines, tableware, vases, ornaments, and decorative items from traditional porcelain manufacturers and shops in Vienna.

4. **Austrian Wines**: Austria's wine regions produce high-quality wines, including Grüner Veltliner, Riesling, Zweigelt, Blaufränkisch, and St. Laurent. Visitors can purchase Austrian wines, wine bottles, wine-related gifts, and souvenirs from local wine shops, wine bars, and wine producers in Vienna.

5. **Dirndl and Lederhosen**: These traditional Austrian garments are popular souvenirs, especially during the Oktoberfest season and cultural events. Visitors can purchase Dirndls (women's dresses) and Lederhosen (men's leather shorts) from boutique shops, department stores, and traditional Austrian clothing stores in Vienna.

6. **Sachertorte**: Sachertorte is a famous Austrian chocolate cake with a layer of apricot jam, covered in dark chocolate icing, and served with whipped cream. Visitors can purchase Sachertorte from Café Sacher and other bakeries in Vienna, packaged in decorative boxes as a sweet souvenir.

7. **Austrian Crystal and Glassware**: Vienna is renowned for its crystal and glassware, including products from famous manufacturers like Swarovski. Visitors can purchase crystal figurines, glassware, jewelry, ornaments, and decorative items from crystal shops, souvenir stores, and specialized retailers in Vienna.

8. **Lipizzaner Horse Souvenirs**: The Lipizzaner horses are a famous Austrian breed known for their grace, beauty, and performance at the Spanish Riding School in Vienna. Visitors can purchase Lipizzaner horse figurines, ornaments, postcards, and souvenirs from gift shops, equestrian stores, and cultural institutions in Vienna.

9. **Viennese Opera Glasses**: Opera glasses are a classic souvenir from Vienna, especially for visitors attending performances at the Vienna State Opera. Visitors can purchase elegant opera glasses, binoculars, and theater accessories from opera shops, gift stores, and cultural institutions in Vienna.

10. **Austrian Jewelry**: Vienna offers a variety of jewelry shops, boutiques, and artisans specializing in Austrian designs, gemstones, metals, and craftsmanship. Visitors can purchase Austrian jewelry, including rings, necklaces, earrings, bracelets, and accessories from local jewelers, designers, and retailers in Vienna.

11. **Viennese Books and Literature**: Vienna has a rich literary heritage, and visitors can purchase books, novels, poetry collections, travel guides, and literature related to Austrian authors, history, culture, and attractions from bookstores, souvenir shops, and cultural institutions in Vienna.

12. **Austrian Beer and Brewery Souvenirs**: Vienna's beer

culture is celebrated through local breweries, beer halls, and craft beer producers. Visitors can purchase Austrian beer, brewery merchandise, beer glasses, coasters, bottle openers, and souvenirs from beer shops, breweries, and pubs in Vienna.

13. **Viennese Art and Prints**: Vienna has a thriving arts scene, with galleries, museums, and artists showcasing paintings, prints, photographs, and artworks inspired by the city's architecture, landmarks, landscapes, and culture. Visitors can purchase Viennese art, prints, posters, and souvenirs from art galleries, exhibitions, and cultural institutions in Vienna.

14. **Austrian Music and Instruments**: Vienna is the "City of Music," and visitors can purchase Austrian music, CDs, DVDs, musical instruments, sheet music, and souvenirs related to classical, jazz, folk, opera, and contemporary Austrian music from music stores, gift shops, and cultural institutions in Vienna.

15. **Viennese Chocolate and Confections**: Vienna's confectionery tradition is celebrated through chocolate shops, patisseries, and dessert cafes offering handmade chocolates, pralines, truffles, pastries, candies, and sweet treats. Visitors can purchase Viennese chocolates, confections, gift boxes, and souvenirs from chocolate shops, bakeries, and cafes in Vienna.

Vienna offers a diverse array of souvenirs that reflect the city's rich history, culture, craftsmanship, culinary delights, and traditions. Whether you're shopping for Mozartkugeln, Viennese coffee, porcelain, wine, traditional garments, crystal, opera glasses, jewelry, books, beer, art, music, chocolate, or other unique souvenirs, Vienna promises a memorable and enjoyable shopping experience for visitors from around the world.

Chapter 9:
Tips For Traveling in Vienna

Traveling to Vienna can be a rewarding experience without breaking the bank if you plan wisely. Here are 15 tips to help you save money and time during your trip to Vienna:

1. **Public Transportation**: Use Vienna's efficient public transportation system, including trams, buses, and the U-Bahn (subway), to navigate the city. Purchase a Vienna Card or a multi-day travel pass for unlimited rides and discounts on attractions.
2. **Vienna Pass**: Consider purchasing the Vienna Pass, which provides access to top attractions, museums, and public transportation. The pass can save you time and money if you plan to visit multiple sites included in the pass.
3. **Free Attractions**: Take advantage of free attractions and activities in Vienna, such as exploring parks, gardens, historic squares, markets, and attending free concerts, festivals, and events.
4. **Museum Discounts**: Visit museums and attractions on designated discount days, evenings, or purchase combination tickets for multiple museums to save money on admission fees.
5. **Walking Tours**: Join free walking tours, guided tours, or self-guided walking routes to explore Vienna's landmarks, architecture, history, and neighborhoods at your own pace without spending extra on transportation or tour fees.
6. **Local Markets**: Shop at local markets, farmers' markets, and grocery stores to purchase fresh produce, snacks, beverages, and ingredients for picnics or meals, saving money on dining out and experiencing local flavors.
7. **Café Culture**: Enjoy Vienna's café culture by visiting traditional coffeehouses, bakeries, and pastry shops for

affordable coffee, pastries, breakfast, snacks, and desserts without dining at expensive restaurants.

8. **Picnics**: Have a picnic in one of Vienna's parks, gardens, squares, or along the Danube River, purchasing local bread, cheese, meats, fruits, vegetables, wine, and snacks from markets or grocery stores to enjoy a budget-friendly meal outdoors.

9. **Accommodation**: Stay in budget-friendly accommodations, hostels, guesthouses, apartments, or book accommodations outside the city center, using public transportation to explore Vienna's attractions, neighborhoods, and landmarks.

10. **Advance Planning**: Research attractions, museums, events, festivals, and activities in Vienna, booking tickets, reservations, tours, and experiences in advance to secure discounts, avoid crowds, and maximize your time and budget.

11. **City Card Benefits**: Utilize the benefits and discounts offered by Vienna's tourist cards, city cards, transport passes, attraction passes, restaurant discounts, shopping promotions, and partner offers available to visitors.

12. **Local Cuisine**: Sample affordable Austrian cuisine, street food, snacks, fast food, and local specialties from food stalls, markets, food trucks, cafes, and casual eateries to experience Viennese flavors without dining at upscale restaurants.

13. **Free Wi-Fi**: Take advantage of free Wi-Fi hotspots, internet cafes, libraries, parks, cafes, and public spaces offering complimentary Wi-Fi access to stay connected, research information, plan activities, and communicate without incurring data roaming charges.

14. **Off-Peak Travel**: Visit Vienna during the off-peak season, shoulder seasons, or weekdays to avoid crowds, secure lower prices on accommodations, flights, attractions, transportation, and experience a more relaxed and affordable trip.

15. **Local Events**: Attend local events, festivals, concerts, performances, exhibitions, markets, fairs, and cultural activities happening in Vienna, exploring free or low-cost entertainment options, experiencing Austrian traditions, and connecting with the local community.

Conclusion

Vienna, the captivating capital of Austria, enthralls visitors with its unrivaled elegance, magnificent architecture, rich cultural scene, and rich history. It is clear that Vienna surpasses expectations and leaves a lasting impression on your heart and soul as you close this travel guide and consider the many experiences, views, sounds, flavors, and memories it has to offer.

Vienna's cobblestone alleys, majestic palaces, innovative coffee shops, lively marketplaces, and peaceful parks all contribute to the city's unique character. These elements weave together a tapestry of legends, customs, inventions, and legacies. Vienna's cultural legacy is resonant with beauty, inventiveness, and significance, from the imperial grandeur of the Hofburg Palace and Schönbrunn Palace to the artistic masterpieces of the Belvedere Museum and Albertina.

Accepting Vienna's reputation as the "City of Music," you can't help but be enthralled with the sounds of famous composers like Strauss, Beethoven, and Mozart resonating in opera houses, theaters, and street corners. A harmonious fusion of artistic brilliance, inventiveness, and passion is fostered by the Vienna Philharmonic Orchestra, Vienna State Opera, Musikverein, and innumerable more venues that showcase classical, opera, jazz, contemporary, and traditional Austrian music.

When you explore Vienna's food scene, you can taste the flavors of Austrian cuisine, which include robust schnitzels, flavorful sausages, creamy strudels, aromatic coffees, fine wines, and delicious pastries, in addition to regional specialties, foreign cuisine, street food, and culinary delights that entice your palate and honor Vienna's culinary legacy.

When you explore Vienna's neighborhoods, you'll come across a variety of districts, quaint squares, bustling markets, gorgeous lanes, hidden treasures, and thriving communities that highlight the city's dynamic fusion of modern elegance and old-world beauty. Vienna's neighborhoods provide distinctive viewpoints, experiences, and tales just waiting to be found, whether you're meandering through the Old Town, visiting the hip Neubau and Leopoldstadt neighborhoods, or finding hidden gems in Wieden, Margareten, and other areas.

Engaging with Vienna's cultural institutions, events, festivals, exhibitions, performances, and traditions, you celebrate the city's artistic vitality, creative spirit, innovative mindset, and commitment to preserving, promoting, and advancing the arts, culture, heritage, and legacy of Vienna and Austria. The city's calendar of events highlights diversity, inclusivity, quality, and enthusiasm. Events include the Vienna Festival, Life Ball, Vienna Jazz Festival, Vienna International Dance Festival, Vienna Coffee Festival, Vienna Design Week, and Vienna Christmas Markets.

As your trip through Vienna comes to a conclusion and you think back on the encounters, memories, friendships, discoveries, and changes that have enhanced your life, you recognize Vienna's capacity to enthrall, inspire, instruct, amuse, and speak to tourists from all over the world. A sense of connection, belonging, and respect for Vienna's contributions to history, culture, art, music, gastronomy, innovation, and the international community are fostered by the city's perennial attraction, hospitality, warmth, and authenticity.

In summary, Vienna continues to be a timeless destination that cuts over boundaries, generations, cultures, and expectations, beckoning visitors to discover, explore, and fully immerse themselves in the alluring spirit, soul, energy, and essence of the city. You leave Vienna with priceless memories, enduring friendships, fresh insights, and a profound admiration for the beauty, charm, grace, elegance, and history of the city. Vienna is a must-visit destination and a place where dreams come true, tales unfold, and magic happens every day because of its enduring impact, influence, inspiration, and significance that resonate with visitors, artists, scholars, adventurers, and dreamers worldwide.

Printed in Great Britain
by Amazon